Back to the Garden

to the

to the Garden

With
Mr
Digwell

© Haynes Publishing, 2009

The right of Paul Peacock to be identified as the author of this Work has been asserted by him in accordance with the Copyright, Designs & Patents Act 1988.

First published in 2009. A catalogue record for this book is available from the British Library

ISBN 978-1-844258-24-6

Published by Haynes Publishing, Sparkford, Yeovil, Somerset BA22 7JJ, UK

Tel: 01963 442030 Fax: 01963 440001 Int. tel: +44 1963 442030 Int. fax: +44 1963 440001

E-mail: sales@haynes.co.uk Website: www.haynes.co.uk

Haynes North America Inc., 861 Lawrence Drive, Newbury Park, California 91320, USA

All images © Mirrorpix

Creative Director: Kevin Gardner

Design and Artwork: David Wildish

Packaged for Haynes by Green Umbrella Publishing

Printed and bound by J F Print Ltd., Sparkford, Somerset

Back to the Garden

to the

With
Mr
Digwell

Written By
Paul Peacock

Back
to the Garden

With
**Mr
Digwell**

Contents

Introducing
Mr Digwell and Patsy

Mr Digwell was born at the age of 65, and so he remained for the next 40 years. Some years he aged by about 20 years and other years he had a miraculous rejuvenation. When he finally got his pension in the late 1980s Mr Digwell had appeared in hundreds of editions of the *Daily Mirror*.

He was just as relevant to the world of striking miners and New Wave pop culture in the 1980s as he had been to the electricity-cut and discontented seventies. His halcyon days were probably spent rebuilding and feeding the country after the Second World War, a process which continued through the 1950s and became a nostalgic influence in the sixties where flat-cap "grandad" allotments went into decline.

His style is that of a didactic uncle who tells you what to do, The Mr Digwell Way is straightforward and easy to understand. In a very few seconds he shows the reader just what to do, and if you follow his instructions you will not go far wrong. Indeed, you're left with the idea that if you don't follow his instructions, he'd have something to say about it.

I did worry that Mr Digwell may not have many friends. But as you read

through the cartoons you find that he also expressed something from the time when gardening also had a social side. He had a competitive side, the grower of champion vegetables, but also had a kind word for his fellow gardener, chatting over the fence. These days we garden alone; but in the past it was about people, and we did it together.

Much of what Mr Digwell has written has changed over the years. Once, like the rest of us, he was happy to use DDT; now he is just as ready to use biological control and advocates a more environmentally friendly mode of gardening. But even in his early days he was groundbreaking in the way he pointed out the value of the birds or how to encourage friendly insects.

Mr Digwell is needed more today than ever. The gardening press, television and radio, cannot show at a glance how to garden as easily as the friendly uncle from way back, a testament to his simple, direct style. He's not pensioned off yet!

Patsy remained a newlywed through her career, which spanned the late 1940s and 1950s. She brought a little homely glamour to the domestic scene, learning how to cook from various family members in a time of great austerity.

Because of this Patsy used reconstituted eggs, which for the sake of our recipes can be replaced by a single fresh one. The hard times of the fourties and fifties meant that the garden became the source of most of Patsy's recipes, and there are definite parallels to modern hard times when more and more people are reaching for home-grown, good quality food.

Mr Digwell's Five Tips for Good Gardening

S o many things have changed over the years that we sometimes don't know where we are. In so many ways what was true when I was young simply doesn't hold up today. But not so in the garden! There might be new plants, new crops, new things such as polytunnels where previously we had to make do with a cloche. But the nitty-gritty of gardening remains as true and valuable today as it ever did. In this section we are going to look at what makes a good gardener.

Good Gardener Tip 1: *Planning*

When you are faced with a blank canvas, probably one covered in weeds and other odds and ends, it is sometimes difficult to imagine what your plot will look like in a year's time. Gardening is no quick fix, more a gradual and methodical process. Don't be overawed by the prospect of hard work, but make a plan that will take you through the plot over a year, or maybe more.

An average allotment-sized vegetable plot can give you nearly all the vegetables you will need, but it takes time to get it to that level of production, so don't race off and then get discouraged.

Tackle the plot in eighths

However large your fresh plot may be, and I am assuming it is new to you here, cover ⅞ of it with black plastic to kill the weeds and simply work on the final ⅛ for now. Draw a plan of the whole plot – where you will put brassicas, beans, peas, salads, potatoes, carrots, turnips and other root crops – and don't forget, leave room in your plan for a double compost heap, some water butts and possibly a shed and a greenhouse.

Next spend your time getting the soil in the first section cleared of weeds,

Modern gardening is more about knowing nature and how it interacts with your crops.

enriched with some good compost and ready for growth. Then you can put something in the soil to grow while you get started on the next eighth.

Use your space wisely

You can fit a lot more into a small space than you might previously have thought. In nature you never see a bare patch of soil, so work out how you can best maintain the planting distances that allow a plant to grow well, without wasting lots of space.

Get used to planting what they used to call cash crops between rows. Runner beans are a favourite of mine for this. Why should you have all that free space inside the wigwam?

Get in there and grow some lettuce, or outdoor tomatoes!

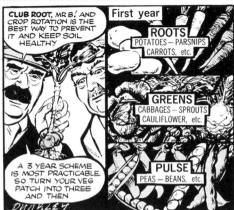

As a general guide, if you start your plot in the *summer*, plant cabbages (buy young plants from the garden centre), carrots, turnips, French beans, peas, potatoes (for Christmas), spinach, spring onions.

If you start your plot in the *autumn*, plant onions, parsley, spinach, turnip, broad beans, rhubarb and any bare-rooted fruit trees.

If you start your plot in the *winter*, plant any bare-rooted fruit trees, rhubarb, onion sets (protect with a cloche), garlic, winter lettuce (protect with a cloche).

If you start your plot in the *spring*, plant well, the whole book is your choice really because a large number of vegetables and fruits are started out in spring.

Crop rotation

Build in a plan for rotating crops so that you do not grow the same plants in the same soil more than once every three years. You have to be sensible about this because crop rotation works best when you are growing on a field scale, less so in just a garden. So take no notice when people say you can prevent clubroot by rotating crops, because you can't; and note carefully what I say about growing onions. What people tell you about growing legumes (plants that get their own nitrogen from the air) to improve the fertility of the soil also misses the point.

The only way to get that nitrogen is to compost the roots, and in any case, some years the legumes take more out of the soil than they take from the air.

But, on the whole, crop rotation is a good way of keeping the soil in good heart.

Possibly the most important crop to avoid growing in the same place twice is the potato. This is because of blight and eelworms, which can build up in the soil. If you plan to move your potatoes around each year, the rest can fill in the space more easily.

Good Gardener Tip 2:
Watching and Listening

Most of the things I know have come from three sources: books, other gardeners who have given me a wonderful amount of information and tips over the years, and comparing my plants with everyone else's to work out why they are different.

There is always something to learn in gardening. For example, I had been growing onions for a long time before I met a chap who grew them completely differently from me. He had a raised bed on which, every November, he had a huge bonfire. It was always the same bed each year, and when the fire cooled down he spread the ashes all over it. Then he covered this with a thin layer of compost and in this he planted his onions. He always grew onions in this bed, nothing else. There was no rotation for him; it was onions in the same bed year after year. But he had the best onions I ever saw. You learn something new every day!

The other thing to do is to simply watch your plants grow. Get to know their ways; they will become a part of you, and that's not some mumbo jumbo. When you see how your plants are growing you will be able to spot things going wrong before they become real problems.

Good Gardener Tip 3: *Look after the Soil*

If you look after your soil it will look after you. Soil must provide water, air and nutrients for your plants and you need to have the ability to change your soil in order to meet the various needs of all the plants you are growing.

Important additives

Lime for making the soil alkaline for growing all your brassica plants. Lime is also important in combating various diseases such as clubroot. If you want rich, wormy soil you will need to add at least a little lime to the soil. Lime is also good at helping turn clay into decent soil.

Sand improves drainage and increases the size of the air spaces in the soil, and is a good way of repairing a wet soil.

Compost is not only full of minerals and nutrients for plants, it also acts as a sponge drawing moisture into the soil. Homemade compost is a good way of getting worms into the soil and when you use it as a mulch it insulates the soil while slowly passing nutrients to your plant's roots.

Peat has been used for a long time for the same sponge-like properties, but its method of extraction has caused environmental problems, and it should be avoided.

Manure is very rich in nutrients and should be kept in big piles until it has rotted down. You know it is ready when there is no smell and the material is friable

HOEING DOES MORE THAN KILL WEEDS,

IT HELPS SOIL TO BRING UP WATER AND AERATES

and easily worked in the fingers. Use it as a way of getting a lot of nutrients into the soil, but be careful not to let it touch the plants because if it is still rotting, it can rot them, too!

Good Gardener Tip 4:
Look after Wildlife

A good gardener looks after the wildlife that visits his garden. Of course there are lots of pests about and we don't need to see our crops eaten away, but I look at it this way: if I could grow a flower that was as beautiful as a goldfinch, it would probably cost me a lot of money.

Leave some spaces for birds, hedgehogs, ladybirds, frogs and toads to get and keep a foothold in the garden. This probably means not using insecticides, but practise getting rid of your pests without chemicals.

If you are completely tidy you will lose out on all kinds of beneficial insects in the garden. A pile of sticks makes a great place for lacewings to spend the winter, and they eat tons of greenfly in the summer. The same goes for ladybirds; and the greenhouse is always a lot healthier if you can have a frog in it.

Good Gardener Tip 5: *Look after Your Tools*

You might have known that I'd prefer wooden shafted tools to anything else. But whatever you buy make sure they are good quality. It is much better to use a good spade than a bad one; you will feel the difference.

Secret tools: In my gardening jacket I have a number of tools I would never be without. My penknife is the first. It is always sharp and ready for doing a bit of deadheading here and there. I also have a dibber – well it was once an old wooden clothes peg.

Then I have a little plastic bag with a wet sponge in it. This is soaked in disinfectant for cleaning my knife and any wounds on plants. Then there is a ball of string for tying plants and separating them from overgrown neighbours.

I have a little set of brightly coloured plastic pegs which I place by plants when I want to remind myself of a job I need to do another day. Finally a notebook and pencil is very valuable for jotting down all the things my fuddled brain cannot remember in the garden.

How to recognize good tools

The shaft of spades and hoes should have the grain running along the length of the wood, which should be made from hickory or ash. The joins for the handle should be smooth and when you hold it you should not feel any ridges or nicks that can cause callouses or cuts.

When you dig with a wooden-handled spade there is some give in the shaft – only a little, but it helps when you are working.

The business end of the tool, where it joins to the shaft, should be seamless with no little nooks and crannies for soil or moisture to collect in, and the securing nut or screw should be substantial enough to hold its position.

Wooden tools needn't have a rubber handle. I am thinking particularly of hoes where the metal ones have a little rubber grip that flies off at the wrong moment.

Care of tools

When you have used your tools they should be cleaned. This doesn't have to take a lot of time; you just wipe away the soil and then plunge the tool a few times into the oil box.

Keep an oil box

This is a bucket filled with sand and then some motor oil. You can use the waste oil from your car's service. Simply plunge the tool blade in and out half a dozen times before you put it away. Always put tools away clean.

Be sharp!

Spades and hoes are cutting tools and since they are cutting through soil they are blunted pretty quickly. At the beginning of each season of use, give your spades and hoes a good sharpen with a flat rasp. Alternatively you can have them professionally sharpened. You will certainly feel the difference using a sharp tool rather than a blunt one.

The right tool for the job

Get used to using the proper tools for the job. Don't just guess what a straight line should be, get a gardener's string on the job and mark it out properly. If you are making raised beds, use a spirit level. One of the most important tools is a dibber for making holes. Don't ever push an onion set or a garlic bulb into the soil, use a dibber!

Balance

My final word on tools! A good tool has a balance, and it causes you to handle it in a certain way. It has a life all of its own and you will enjoy using it.

Growing Vegetables

Artichokes - *The poshest vegetables on the plot*

Globe artichokes - *The thistle you can eat*

I love to grow globe artichokes because they make such a fantastic display on the vegetable plot. They are the tallest herbaceous plants in the garden. Each spring give them a good mulch of well-rotted manure. In the first year don't take any 'chokes at all, but leave them on the plant to mature. This will give you a much better harvest the next year.

Modern varieties of artichokes are very different from when I started gardening. The individual bracts, the little fat leaves you pick off the flower to eat, have very tender skins.

During the summer you should never let the plant get dry, and it must be kept in a very sunny site. I tend to feel the soil, and if it begins to turn dry give it a good watering. You can add a little organic fertilizer for an extra boost just as the 'chokes are developing.

The globe artichoke is actually a giant thistle with tough little bracts, though when cooked well and dipped into sauce are fun to eat. Don't fall into the trap of picking globe artichokes too late. The older the flowers the tougher the chew.

JERUSALEM ARTICHOKES, THE NO-STARCH VEGETABLE... ...IDEAL FOR WEIGHT WATCHERS!

PLANT TUBERS NOW TILL MARCH, 6 INCHES DEEP, 3 FEET APART

FOLIAGE GROWS SEVERAL FEET, MAKES A HANDY WIND-BREAK

KEEP WEEDS AT BAY – LIFT AS REQUIRED FROM NOVEMBER ONWARDS

GLOBE ARTICHOKES! TAKE SUCKERS FROM MATURE PLANTS IN APRIL

PLANT THEM 2 FEET APART

THE FEATHERY FOLIAGE IS GREAT FOR FLOWER ARRANGING

HARVEST FLOWER HEADS FOR EATING BEFORE THEY ARE FULLY OPEN

REALLY TASTY!

Modern varieties:

Green Globe – *easiest to grow*
Romanesco – *purple*
Violetta Precoce

Jerusalem artichokes - *Neither an artichoke nor a potato*

I love Jerusalem artichokes, but not everyone does, so try a few before you dedicate soil space to them. Their real name is Girasole, or Italian sunflowers, and they produce a tuber that is low in starch. The name 'Jerusalem' came from a mispronunciation of its real name and they are called artichokes because they taste a little like the globe. Treat them almost the same way as potatoes but they grow very tall and you do not harvest your tubers until November from a spring planting. They need good rich soil and never let the plants go dry. Add a little general-purpose liquid fertilizer to the water once a week.

They grow to become an enormous plant, so make sure there is plenty of space between them, and when they are around a foot tall (30cm) earth them up just like potatoes.

Harvest just like potatoes, wash the tubers and store them in a cool, dry, dark place.

Modern varieties

Fuseau – *the most popular and least knobbly of them all. This is probably the only one you will find these days.*

Asparagus - *The complete English vegetable*

Many years ago the French asparagus variety 'Argenteuil' was widely available and you could buy crowns that were easy to get a crop from, even in their first year. Alas, like most things these days, our choices are limited and you now have to grow for three years before getting a good crop with the varieties we have available. On the positive side, however, modern varieties have a better disease resistance and they are more tolerant of both drought and low nutrient levels.

Everything I wrote about asparagus remains true today. You have to dig a long trench inside which you make a little mound. Over this the roots are spread and you fill the pit with good quality compost. Firm the plants in at around 18in to 2ft apart (45–60cm) and keep them watered. During the summer feed weekly with an organic fertilizer and make sure the

soil never dries out. In autumn the fronds will die back – compost them. Then mulch the trench with a thick layer of well-rotted manure and compost mixed in equal volumes. Repeat this for the second year, and in the third year take only half the spears. In the following years take about 75% of them, leaving the rest to grow to make next year's crop.

In the spring we start thinking about sowing seeds and planting crops. One of the terrible problems that people just don't think about is the way we handle plants. We grow them indoors and in greenhouses where they are cosy and warm and then, when the threat of frosts is subsiding, we throw them into cold soil.

All vegetable plants react to this shock by growing a few wood cells for protection, and the result is that the crop is tougher than it should be.

Warm the soil before you transplant by spreading black plastic on the ground for a couple of weeks before you plan to put your plants outside.

Another important tip is to keep a can full of water in the greenhouse. You don't fancy a cold shower I'm sure; neither do your plants.

Beetroot -
The vegetable cricket was invented for

Since I started growing beetroot as a very young lad, so much has changed. We used to take the beets only once they were big enough and boil them, sometimes pickle them and I must confess to enjoy eating them raw. But we never thought to eat the leaves as salad, nor of growing them to pick fresh long before the roots were ready to bulb out.

These days beetroot, and all its wonderfully coloured cousins, are used in their entirety.

Beetroot can be sown as thickly as you like, thinning them out to about 2in (5cm) and using these sproutings in stir-fry dishes or salads. Some people blend them into juice drinks. Then after a few weeks you can thin them to about 4in (10cm) and use these larger thinnings in salads. You can sow beetroots from April all the way to August and expect some kind of a crop in November.

Beetroot will not germinate when there is a frost on the ground. It is better to sow on days after the frost has passed. Birds love beet seedlings, so gently cover them with horticultural fleece when very young, removing it to water and feed. When you have thinned out to 4in (10cm) you can remove the fleece for good.

FISH AND BEETROOT HASH

ONE OF THE AMERICAN BOYS TOLD ME ABOUT THIS

MIX TOGETHER A GOOD TEACUPFUL OF FLAKED COOKED FISH

THE SAME OF CHOPPED, NOT MASHED, COOKED POTATO

AND A MEDIUM SIZED CHOPPED COOKED BEETROOT

SEASON WITH:-

ONION FLAVOURING

A LITTLE MIXED HERBS

SALT & PEPPER

AND A TEASPOONFUL OF YOUR FAVOURITE SAUCE

MOISTEN WITH A TABLE-SPOONFUL OR SO OF MILK

AND FRY IN A LITTLE FAT

WHEN WELL-BROWNED UNDERNEATH, FOLD OVER LIKE AN OMELETTE

GOOD WAY TO USE BEET-ROOT TOO!

Modern varieties include:

Bolthardy – *the most common easy grow beetroot*
Burpee's Golden – *a golden variety, pretty coloured and very tasty*
Pablo – *this one looks as though it is wrapped in silk*

Plants in the winter - *No time to rest in the greenhouse*

Winters have always been unpredictable. You never can really work out which ones are going to be warm and which will make your moustache freeze. It's a good job because we'd have nothing to complain about.

Many plants are hardy enough to withstand the cold, but constant rocking in the wind can be a serious problem for some. Brussels sprouts in particular need a good firming-in with

the heel at the base of the plant. If they are allowed to rock the sprouts burst open and are almost useless. So, if you want firm sprouts, dig your heels in as they cope with the worst of the November weather.

Many plants such as broccoli and late salads like chard, or all-the-year-round lettuce need little more protection than a spray of water on nights where there's a milk frost. As the water freezes the ice insulates the plant from the worst of the colder air.

Horticultural fleece is excellent for making a cosy little bed for plants to keep warm underneath. It allows light to penetrate, even rain, but it does make an effective barrier from the cold. Newspaper also works, but it is not so pretty, is more shading and goes soggy when wet. Also, on windy days your plant blanket can be found blown all over the neighbourhood.

Any time in the winter is a good time to disinfect the greenhouse and don't forget the glass. Strong winds will send it flying into next door's plot.

Brassicas - *The family that fills the garden*

Brassicas are a family of plants that have flowers in the shape of a cross of four petals and come in all shapes and sizes. They are probably the most important vegetables on the plot.

Cabbage is fundamental to the vegetable garden and over the years we have grown it in many ways. More people write to me about cabbage than any other vegetable, mostly because the whole country is now suffering with clubroot, a horrid fungal infection that twists and gnarls at the roots.

You only have to walk on the soil with the spores on your boots to spread it around and once it is in your soil it can be many years before you get rid of it – if ever!

You can buy a chemical to counter the fungus but I prefer to get good strong plants in the ground first and treat them with a lot of lime. Here's how I do it.

Plants need water to live, but few of them need what we used to call 'wet feet'.

Water promotes fungal infections otherwise known as rot or botrytis.

It is a good idea to incorporate a handful of sand when you plant your vegetables.

WINTER GREENHOUSE DRILL (1)

HAD A LECTURE FROM OLD DIGWELL TODAY ABOUT THE GREENHOUSE

GREEN SLIME (ALGAE) SOMETIMES DEVELOPS ON POT BOTTOMS—IT MUST BE WIPED OFF

AND ANY ON THE TOP SOIL REMOVED

BREAK THE SURFACE LIGHTLY. THIS'LL ENCOURAGE ROOT ACTION

KEEP THE GLASS LIGHTS CLEAN

YOU'LL WANT ALL THE LIGHT YOU CAN GET FROM THE WEAK WINTER SUN

VENTILATE DAILY AS WEATHER PERMITS, IF YOU DON'T YOU MAY GET MILDEW

AVOID DRAUGHTS BY OPENING LIGHTS ON THE LEE SIDE OF THE GREENHOUSE

TRY TO KEEP A *LEVEL* TEMPERATURE OF 45°F. AT NIGHT

Sow your seeds into 3in (8cm) pots and let them germinate in early spring in the normal way. Pinch them out, then rather than planting them out in April or May, keep them growing in the pot until June. By this time the roots will be really well established and you just have to keep them watered.

In mid-June use a bulb planter and cut out a plug of soil. Sprinkle a good handful of lime all over the surface of the hole. Be very generous with the lime. Then partly fill with good rich compost that has been bought from the garden centre and has no clubroot in

> YOU WANT TO HEEL OVER THEM **BROCCOLI** PLANTS TO PROTECT 'EM AGAINST THE FROST, MR B... **HEY!** I DON'T MEAN **JUMP** ON 'EM!

> **SOME** PEOPLE!— WHAT I MEAN IS, LAY 'EM DOWN LIKE THIS, AND MAKE SURE THE HEADS POINT NORTH

> **CAULIFLOWERS?** TIE IN THE LEAVES WITH A STRAND OF RAFFIA— IT'LL HELP KEEP THE CURDS FROM GETTIN' SPOILED

> — AND, WARMIN' TO ME FROST THEME, REMEMBER **STANDARD ROSE TREES** ARE LIKELY TO COP IT MORE FROM COLD THAN BUSH OR DWARF TREES —THEY'RE MORE EXPOSED—SO COVER 'EM LIKE THIS...

> AND DON'T FORGET YOUR PET **MARROW.** PROTECT IT WITH NEWSPAPERS AND CANES LIKE THIS

> IF YOU'VE GOT ANY TENDER YOUNG SHRUBS YOU'RE NOT SURE ABOUT, SURROUND 'EM WITH LAUREL OR OTHER EVERGREEN BRANCHES

> AND IF YOUR GREENHOUSE ISN'T HEATED, NEWSPAPERS WILL PROTECT FROM A SLIGHT FROST

it. Plant your cabbages in this. Their roots will be well developed, the lime reduces the effect of the fungus and the cabbage will be hardly touched.

Walk the plank

Get into the habit of never walking on your soil and be fastidious about cleaning your boots. More disease is spread about the garden by people and their feet than anything else. It isn't too much effort to have a bucket of disinfectant to stand your wellies in either!

All brassicas like to be well firmed into the soil. If they can rock about they either run to seed or they grow loose. This is particularly important when it comes to growing broccoli, when the sprouts will explode into little leaves if the plant is not well firmed in.

If you can make a ball of soil and it holds its shape, it is too wet. Add some broken crocks to leafy crops.

Root crops in damp soil are best grown with a drain ditch next to each row. Building high raised beds also reduces excess water.

Spring Cabbage -
Leaf green or balled up – spring cabbage is simple

These are the easiest plants to grow, but take a little time and they need a little protection in the winter. I usually sow them in pots from late May onwards so I have plants big enough for transplanting by the end of June, following the same regime to beat clubroot as for all cabbages.

You can also sow spring cabbage directly into the soil, thinning them out as required.

The funny thing about cabbages is they grow differently according to how much room they have. Space them at 1ft (30cm) for greens but if you want them to ball up like other cabbages, space them at least 18in (45cm) or even as far apart as 2ft (60cm) for Savoy 'King'.

You should aim to get

Think small: Don't over fill your spade, if it takes a little longer what does it matter?

Keep your back straight: You use the muscles in your arms and legs to dig, not your back. Keep it straight and keep well.

Planting: Once you have turned the soil and broken it up a little, use the lighter hoe to make it ready for planting.

your plants in the ground by mid-July and firm them well into the soil. Give them a feed of soluble fertilizer once during August, but no more: you want this plant to grow slowly.

Choose a sunny spot that is not exposed to wind, for it is the driving wind and rain that causes them a problem in the winter. Good varieties are Savoy King, Primo Cabbage and Savoy Siberia which is the best for those living in high altitudes or in the north.

Make sure the soil is free-draining because nothing causes more trouble than standing water; spring cabbage does not like to get its feet wet. Apart from that, they're easy!

Did you know that cabbages were introduced into this country by the Romans. They escaped their gardens and became what we know now as 'wild cabbage'. Wherever there was a Roman settlement, wild cabbages can be found in abundance. The Romans brought many food plants into the UK, including stinging nettles. They were so cold here in Britain they used to beat their legs with nettles to make them feel warm. What men!

When people think about gardens they worry about digging. They needn't. The secret to digging is having a good, sharp spade. Make sure you buy the spade that feels right for you and if you're a lady, don't choose a large one.

It is more important not to get injured by digging up too much soil because then you won't be able to dig at all.

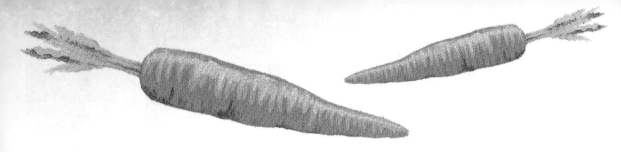

Carrots

The easiest crop in the garden, you can sow them from April right through to the end of August and have a good crop almost all the year round. The big problem is that they don't like rough, stony or nutrient rich soil.

For carrots preparation is the thing. You can use soil that grew a crop like beans or cabbage last year, but you have to work the soil. Get the hoe out and chop away until the soil is like porridge before you add liquid to it, completely crumbly with no lumps. Then you can sow your seeds.

There are carrots to suit every taste these days, but I still prefer 'Nantes Early'.

An excellent trick I picked up from exhibition gardeners is to grow carrots in a drainpipe. You cut the drainpipe into 3ft (1m) lengths and then cut it in half lengthways. Tape the pipe together and stop up one end. Then fill this with a 50:50 mixture of sand and compost and sow your seeds in this. The carrot will grow as long as you keep it watered. When it is time to show your carrots, carefully un-tape the drainpipe and you should have 3ft-long carrots, tapering to a fine point.

Modern varieties include:

Chantenay – *a great variety, good and sweet*
Autumn King – *good for sowing late summer*
Nantes – *good for sowing in spring*

Skins or not?

The main reason we peel vegetables is because we used to spray them with chemicals that stay on the outside. But if you grow them organically you can simply wash your carrots and roast them with the skins on – it's a whole new experience!

Cauliflowers - *The flowers you can eat*

Why people don't find cauliflowers easy I cannot fathom. They are just as easy as cabbages as long as you follow the rules.

They need to be treated like cabbages and then not allowed to grow too large, protected from the weather and insects and harvested quickly. When I first started growing caulis we used to stagger the sowings in order to get a decent crop over a long period, otherwise you couldn't eat them all before they went off. Now I sow a couple of rows and freeze them; it's much easier to keep them perfect in the freezer than in the soil.

You can have cauliflowers almost all the year round if you like, and they come in two

varieties – summer and winter. The winter types are more closely related to broccoli.

Summer and autumn caulis are sown indoors in January in pots to transplant like cabbages in April. Winter caulis are planted in pots in May to be planted out by July.

They suffer from cabbage-root fly even more than cabbages do, so buy those little discs that stop the blighters getting to the stem where it touches the soil.

Modern varieties include:

Summer and autumn: **Kestrel** – *very strong grower, good curds*
Serac F1 – *very early*
Winter and spring: **Needles F1, Foreland F1**

Celeriac - *The root that tastes of celery*

It is wonderful to grow your own vegetables because you begin, after a little while, to tell the difference between fresh veg straight from the ground and that sitting around in the shops for days on end. Celeriac is one of the best ones to grow because the fresh stuff tastes so much better than the bought.

To grow celeriac you have to start plants off indoors, sowing in March and keeping them growing in 3in (8cm) pots of compost until late April. Thin them to one plant per pot. Meanwhile, dig a trench about a spade and a half deep and half-fill it with a 50:50 mixture of rich compost and very well-rotted manure and fill the rest of it with the soil

you dug out. These are hungry plants. Then you carry on as in the illustrations. The most widely available variety is 'Monarch'.

You can make life in the kitchen easier if you lift your celeriac a couple of days early and bury them in sand. It makes the skin a little easier to peel and they sweeten even more than ever. If you grow them in a 50:50 mixture of manure and compost they come out quite clean too.

Celery - *The dental stick*

This way of growing celery has been around since Victorian times, and it never fails. Any plant that has to make strong flavours needs a lot of nutrients. Otherwise they would not be able to make those complex chemicals in the first place. Celery is no exception, and the nutrients are provided by the manure in the trench. Also the manure continues to rot a bit, keeping the celery roots snug in the soil.

Sow in trays or modules of compost indoors in March and transplant them in May. They will be ready in late summer.

Modern varieties include:

Loretta – *self-blanching plants, you don't need to earth them up*

Celery Granada – *excellent disease resistance*

Celery has nothing but water and flavour.

There are very few calories in a stick of celery, so few that it takes more energy

> " *You use more energy by digesting celery than you get out of it, but it's full of vitamins and it tastes wonderful.* "

to eat it than you get from it. The flavours in the plant make celery a perfect condiment for soups and stews and make an excellent addition to a curry as well as a salad, which is how I like to eat them best. They are particularly good for the complexion.

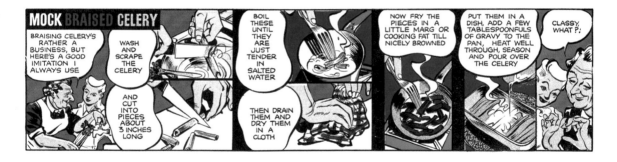

Swiss chard - *You can eat all of this plant – it's fantastic*

This plant is really a beet, better than spinach in many respects, being easier to grow and just as good for you. Sow them in the soil where they are to grow, which doesn't have to be particularly rich. Thin them out as described below and keep them weed free and that's almost all there is to it. You should sow from April onwards and every fortnight until mid-May. This way you should get a decent crop until the end of the year. From November onwards you can cover them with a cloche, which will extend their usefulness until Christmas.

The leaves should be picked off and used almost straight away. You can cook the stalks as though they were asparagus and the leaves as though they were spinach. One thing about spinach is that it gets too rich if grown on rich soil; this never happens with chard. And of course, the leaves are brightly coloured – but I don't know what I was thinking when I suggested you use them for flower arranging!

Beets and Brassicas

There is a world of difference between beets, with their thick leaves and easy to grow habits and the cabbage family otherwise known as brassicas. Beets are easier to grow than brassicas and yet you can more or less do anything with the leaves you can do with cabbages.

If you only have a little space I would suggest you grow beets, chard, everlasting spinach and so on rather than cabbages – if all you want are leaves of course. You cannot get a cauliflower or a sprout alternative, but the leaves are brilliant.

Beet leaves work in salads, especially if you take them when they are young in a way that cabbage cannot. The leaves are sweeter and there isn't that aftertaste that you get with cabbage leaves. You can use beet leaves in dishes like coleslaw instead of white cabbage too.

There are two reasons for using beets instead of cabbage in any

garden. Firstly you can use the vein in the centre of the old leaves as a dipping vegetable. It is super with homemade cottage cheese, pickles and more exotic dips like hummus.

The other reason for using chard and beets is that you get such fantastic colours! What a brilliant salad with every colour of the rainbow! They keep their colour a little when boiled if you put a pinch of bicarbonate of soda in the boiling water.

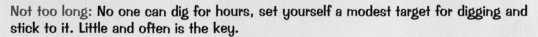

Digging Tips

When people think about gardens they worry about digging. They needn't. The secret to digging is having a good, sharp spade. Make sure you buy the spade that feels right for you and if you're a lady, don't choose a large one.

It is more important not to get injured by digging up too much soil because then you won't be able to dig at all.

Think small: Don't over fill your spade, if it takes a little longer what does it matter?

Not too long: No one can dig for hours, set yourself a modest target for digging and stick to it. Little and often is the key.

Tilth: We dig in order to aerate the soil and make it crumbly ready for sowing and planting. Once you have turned the soil and broken it up a little, use the lighter hoe to make it ready for planting.

Chicory - *The strong flavoured leaves*

Forty years ago there was only one way to grow chicory but these days we are all much more used to bitter-flavoured leaves in salads, so there isn't much need to blanch them in the same way. Sow them in June and you will have some lovely leaves to pull in November – just right to mix with lettuce and rocket. You can add some dandelion leaves too.

Thin them out as I suggested years ago and simply let them grow. You can put the plants that are growing under a pot, and protect with a cloche in really bad weather. Some people bring the roots indoors in pots of compost. Do this in December – anywhere will do, but I keep mine in the shed where there is some light but not too much.

The French make a coffee substitute from chicory roots by drying them completely and grinding them to make a powder. The roots can also be eaten boiled or roasted. I like to cut them into very small pieces and roast a few amongst carrots and parsnips.

Modern varieties include:

Apollo – *an old fashioned forcing variety*
Palla Rosa – *a leaf-picking modern variety*
You can often find chicory in salad leaf mixes and the very popular micro-salad

" Today everyone buys mixed salad and eats it from a large bowl. Chicory is a great ingredient, as are endive and beets. When I was a boy we used to grow dandelions in rows too – they make a great early spring salad ingredient. "

Root crops: All roots can be stored under ground. Dry your roots and tubers. Dig a big hole and line it with six inches of straw. Lay your roots on this and cover with more straw. On top of the straw put a good layer of earth. This is called a clamp.

Carrots, beets and turnips can be laid in dry sand in boxes. Swedes and parsnips can be simply left where they are growing.

Cucumber - *It is strange that most gardeners grow tomatoes but not cucumbers*

There are two distinct types, smooth and ridge. Ridge cucumbers are easy to grow and produce smaller fruits. Whichever type you grow, you will find home grown the best!

Greenhouse cucumbers

The fruit appears on side shoots. Traditional plants have male and female flowers. Do not allow them to pollinate, otherwise the fruits will be bitter. Remove the male flowers – these are the ones that do not have a little bump behind the flower.

F1 hybrids only produce female flowers, so you don't have to worry about them, but they need warmer conditions at around 18°C. They also need support.

Outdoor cucumbers

Outdoor types are hardier and will grow as little bushes. You can grow them indoors to get an even better crop. These too produce male flowers that have to be removed.

Sowing

All cucumbers can be sown in 3in (8cm) pots. Sow two seeds per pot and discard the weakest. They need 20°C to germinate. Sow them in April.

Greenhouse varieties should be potted onto their final bed when they have two true leaves. They need plenty of compost and give them a good deep mulch of compost on top of this. This is one plant that needs humidity – so water the paths. Feed them like tomatoes. Keep on picking the fruit otherwise the plant will start to die.

Walk the plank:
Stop walking on the soil. Your boots spread disease everywhere. This is the reason why clubroot is everywhere. If you lay a plank and only walk on this you will cut out a lot of disease.

Don't compost:
Never compost diseased material. Burn it first and then add this to the compost heap. Make sure the heap gets really hot to kill any disease.

Disinfect:
If you are pruning, always disinfect the secateurs regularly. Clean knives and utensils regularly, dipping them in disinfectant. Clean your pots every year.

Outdoor cucumbers should be spaced at 2ft (60cm) in very rich soil. If you can protect them with a cloche all the better. Mulch heavily and then treat as greenhouse plants for feeding and watering.

Marrows - *Versatile and tasty*

These are hungry, thirsty plants which used to be fussy, but now are much less so. You can dig a trench and fill it with manure if you like but there is a better way which works especially if you don't have much room.

Normally you sow two seeds in a 3in (8cm) pot and discard the weakest growing plant. You can do this any time between March and the end of May. Leave the pot on the windowsill to grow, or pop it in the greenhouse and then from May onwards transplant the seedlings into a growbag. Keep the compost moist but not too wet. Once a week feed with tomato fertilizer to the correct dilution. Male and female flowers will form. You can tell the difference between the two because female flowers have tiny marrows just behind the flower.

You can fertilize the female flowers if you like by pulling the male flowers off and brushing the pollen onto the female ones.

The modern way to harvest these plants is to take young fruits and use them as courgettes and then allow maybe one per plant to grow out to become a full-blown marrow.

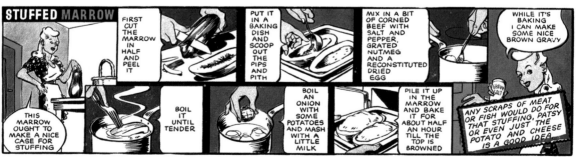

STUFFED MARROW

THIS MARROW OUGHT TO MAKE A NICE CASE FOR STUFFING

FIRST CUT THE MARROW IN HALF AND PEEL IT

PUT IT IN A BAKING DISH AND SCOOP OUT THE PIPS AND PITH

MIX IN A BIT OF CORNED BEEF WITH SALT AND PEPPER, GRATED NUTMEG AND A RECONSTITUTED DRIED EGG

WHILE IT'S BAKING I CAN MAKE SOME NICE BROWN GRAVY

BOIL IT UNTIL TENDER

BOIL AN ONION WITH SOME POTATOES AND MASH WITH A LITTLE MILK

PILE IT UP IN THE MARROW AND BAKE IT FOR ABOUT HALF AN HOUR TILL THE TOP IS BROWNED

ANY SCRAPS OF MEAT OR FISH WOULD DO FOR THAT STUFFING, PATSY OR EVEN JUST THE POTATO AND CHEESE IS A GOOD IDEA

Panel 1: HERE'S HOW TO GO ABOUT GETTING AS FINE A **MARROW** AS EVER GOT CHRISTENED BY MISTAKE ROUND HARVEST FESTIVAL TIME, MR N!...

Panel 2: JUST TO MAKE SURE LATE FROSTS DON'T COP THE PLANTS, COVER 'EM THE FIRST FEW NIGHTS

Panel 3: WHEN THE FLOWERS APPEAR, ENSURE GOOD RESULTS BY POLLINATING THE FEMALE BLOOM [THE ONE WITH THE TINY MARROW ATTACHED]...

Panel 4: AS THE PLANTS DEVELOP, FEED 'EM WEEKLY WITH DILUTED LIQUID MANURE, A GALLON A PLANT, OR LIQUID DRIED BLOOD SOLUTION, 6 PINTS A PLANT

Panel 5: KEEP THE FRUIT LIFTED...THIS WAY THEY'LL GET MORE SUN ON 'EM AND WILL STAY CLEAN AND FREE FROM SOIL PESTS

... BY PRESSING THE PICKED, HALF-DAY OLD, MALE BLOOM INTO IT, GIVING IT A LITTLE TWIST TO DISLODGE THE POLLEN

DUNKLEY

PICKLED MARROW

I MUST NOT WASTE THE REST OF DAD'S MARROW – THINK I'LL PICKLE IT – WHERE'S MRS A?

PEEL AND CUT UP THE MARROW IN CUBES – WEIGH 2lbs. SPRINKLE THEM WELL WITH SALT AND LEAVE FOR AN HOUR

BOIL 1½ PINTS OF VINEGAR WITH 6 CLOVES AND 1 DOZ. PEELED SHALLOTS OR PICKLING ONIONS FOR 10 MIN.

ADD THE **DRAINED** MARROW CUBES AND BOIL FOR 20 MIN.

NOW ADD ¼ lb. LUMP SUGAR, LET IT DISSOLVE

THEN ½ OZ OF TURMERIC AND 1 OZ MUSTARD POWDER MIXED TO A PASTE WITH A LITTLE COLD VINEGAR

BOIL TOGETHER FOR ANOTHER 10 MIN. THEN POT AND COVER

Modern varieties include:

Badger Cross – *true marrows that do well as courgette replacements when small*

Onions and air crops: Onions, shallots and garlic need to be dried out and their skins hardened in the air. This is referred to as curing.

Endive - *Frizzy bitter salad*

I think we used to make gardening too difficult years ago. Perhaps because we have a much wider selection of fruit and vegetables in the shops we want to grow more too. I now sow endive in the spring and right through to the end of August so I have a supply from very early summer to Christmas. We are getting used to the flavour more too, so I don't blanch every plant. A mixed bowl of salad leaves might have some blanched leaves and some normal leaves along with umpteen other salad leaves too.

Endive seeds are very small and you don't have to plant them in rows. Some people make a raised bed with patches of salads, some lettuce here, chicory there and endive too. They are also really good for pot-growing, which is a very convenient way of keeping the crop healthy

over the winter – just bring it indoors. Water them regularly, never let them dry out, and feed them with some liquid fertilizer once a fortnight.

Modern varieties include:

Indivia D'Estale A Cuore Giallo
Salad King – *probably the best one*

Warming the soil

In the spring we start thinking about sowing seeds and planting crops. One of the terrible problems that people just don't think about is the way we handle plants.

We grow them indoors and in greenhouses where they are cosy and warm and then, when the threat of frosts is subsiding, we throw them into cold soil.

All vegetable plants react to this shock by growing a few wood cells for protection, and the result is that the crop is tougher than it should be.

Warm the soil before you transplant by spreading black plastic on the ground for a couple of weeks before you plan to put your plants outside.

French beans

These plants are wonderful grown on the plot rather than bought in the shops. You will never want to buy them again! Also they are so easy to grow. First-timers and people with little space, will do best with the dwarf varieties as the climbers grow over 6ft (1.8m) tall and need support.

Plant the beans outside (as in the cartoon) in mid-May, when there is no chance of frost. You could plant them in mid-April in the greenhouse or a polytunnel or with a cloche over them.

I always find it useful to lay some black plastic on the soil in April to help it warm up. We could never do this years ago, so beans had to be planted in June. You are looking for a warm soil because these beans aren't really French at all – they come from the tropics.

You will find, if you keep them well watered, that even the dwarf beans will droop onto the ground, so give them a bit of a lift with some pea sticks.

The big secret is: nutrients and water. Don't be put off by watering them

every day and feeding them every week. That way you will get very tasty pods, and if you continue to pick them you will have a continual supply because more flowers will appear to replace those harvested.

Modern varieties include:

Twiggy – *these are thin ones – very posh on the plate but tasty*
Masterpiece – *early maturing*
Prince – *the best all rounder*

Use a water bottle: You can make an emergency watering for a group of plants by filling a large plastic lemonade bottle with water and piercing the side in three places, equally spaced.

Control the flow of the dribbling water by loosening the cap.

Stand it amongst the plants and it will water a set of plants for a day.

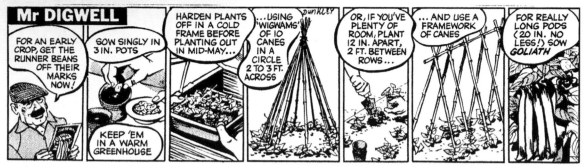

Mr DIGWELL

FOR AN EARLY CROP, GET THE RUNNER BEANS OFF THEIR MARKS NOW!

SOW SINGLY IN 3 IN. POTS

KEEP 'EM IN A WARM GREENHOUSE

HARDEN PLANTS OFF IN A COLD FRAME BEFORE PLANTING OUT IN MID-MAY...

...USING 'WIGWAMS' OF 10 CANES IN A CIRCLE 2 TO 3 FT. ACROSS

OR, IF YOU'VE PLENTY OF ROOM, PLANT 12 IN. APART, 2 FT. BETWEEN ROWS...

... AND USE A FRAMEWORK OF CANES

FOR REALLY LONG PODS (20 IN. NO LESS!) SOW GOLIATH

Runner beans

These plants need nutrients, water and a good head start! I have tried many different ways of growing them from seed and starting them in pots indoors is by far the best way. If you sow them directly in their growing positions the mice get them.

Dig the soil beforehand and incorporate as much organic material as you can. Beans are legumes and 'fix' nitrogen from the air into the soil themselves. The extra nitrogen will give luxuriant growth, but not many more pods. However I always believe the healthier the plant the better the fruit. The other thing you need to be sure of is a free draining soil. If you have waterlogged soil you need to improve the drainage to grow runner beans properly.

When the plants set fruit, make sure they never suffer from water stress. I water every two days and feed once a week. This way you will get the fullest, tastiest pods.

They are quite frost hardy and you can sow another batch in late September to get fruit in the spring.

Modern varieties include:

Imperial Green – *a good all-rounder*
Aquadulce
Express

Garlic - *The aromatic life saver!*

Garlic is a wonderful plant that has served mankind for centuries. Before the discovery of penicillin the government paid farmers a shilling a punnet to grow garlic, which was used to make special bandages that stopped infections. These were used on the battlefields and hospitals and so many soldiers owed their lives to the little garlic, but never thought to eat it afterwards!

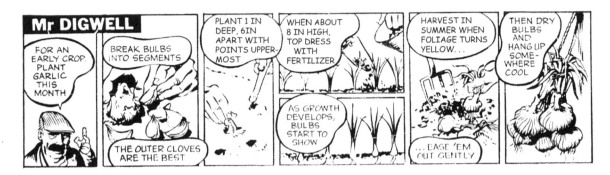

Put garlic into a sunny position with well draining soil and it will grow quickly. Too much water will make the garlic bulbs rot, but it does not like to dry out either. A spade of sand and a spade of well-rotted manure is perfect.

Garlic should be planted in October, but you will get away with planting as late as January. It is very hardy and actually improves in very cold weather. Do not plant garlic for eating from the supermarket, though I do use these corms for growing as a protective layer around the plants. Garlic for eating should be bought specially for the purpose and planted flat bottom down at a depth of 2in (5cm). Use a dibber to make the holes, not your finger or the corm itself, and once planted cover and firm in. They have a tendency to pop out as the root grows, so keep an eye on them.

Space them at 4in (10cm) and there should be 15in (50cm) between the rows. Feed

Use the hoe:
My grandfather taught me this. You hoe up the soil around the plant and the heat of the day will 'draw' water from below.

Even on the driest times there is a lot of water deep under the soil surface and if we can attract this to the roots all the better.

When you're really desperate:
Use a pair of scissors to cut down the leaf area, thus reducing the evaporation load on the plant itself – but this really is a last resort.

them once a month with a liquid feed and in April give them a mulch of fresh compost. The only care they need is to be weed free and fed regularly. They are hungry plants because they have a lot of chemicals to manufacture that gives their strong flavour. If you grow garlic in containers make sure they are at least 6in (18cm), though I have grown them in drinks containers quite successfully.

Do not save garlic you have grown from year to year because they pick up diseases and your crop will diminish.

FOR A MAN WHO LIKES HIS ROAST BEEF, I'M SURPRISED YOU HAVEN'T PLANTED OUT YOUR **HORSERADISH** YET, MR NEWCOMBE

I SHOULD'VE GOT ON TO YOU IN FEBRUARY ABOUT THAT... NEVER MIND, THERE'S STILL JUST TIME TO...

...MAKE GOOD-SIZED HOLES WITH A DIBBER, 9 INCHES APART IN A BED OF WELL-DUG, FAIRLY RICH SOIL

...INTO THESE, DROP THE PIECES OF ROOT 8-9 INCHES LONG

...AND COVER 'EM WITH 3-4 INCHES OF SOIL

FOR BEST RESULTS LIFT THE ROOTS EVERY ALTERNATE FEBRUARY...

...THROWING AWAY THOSE YOU DON'T WANT AND REPLANTING THE BED

HORSERADISH CAN SPREAD LIKE MAD, SO BE SURE TO GET RID OF THE TINIEST BITS OF ROOT OR EACH ONE WILL GROW INTO A PLANT

Horseradish -
The hottest British vegetable

This plant would otherwise be called a perennial weed if it wasn't for the roots that are used to make the hottest sauce there is. If you leave even the tiniest bit of root in the soil it will grow to become a huge plant and unchecked it will take over the entire garden.

Horseradish is bought in winter and planted in fairly rich soil as soon as you get it home. The leaves grow quite large and they can be harvested and used as a green manure. Some people dig a hole a foot across and lay the root in place, filling with rich compost. Either way the plant will burst through the soil in spring.

Harvesting is easy. In November, or whenever the leaves start to look a bit messy because of the cold, dig up the plants using a fork so you don't damage them. Cut off the leaves and divide the roots, keeping the bigger portion for yourself and replant the smaller parts for new growth.

Spacing vegetables:
A drill is a straight line scraped in the earth to the depth of your little finger.
Most rows are an arm's length apart. Double rows (beans) are a cubit from the finger to the elbow apart.

Carrots, turnips, beets, celery and most salads are spaced at a span apart, but you have to thin them out to get to this. (A span is the distance from the thumb and the little finger stretched out.)

Potatoes, cabbages, sprouts, cauliflowers are all spaced at a cubit apart.

Leeks - *You just cannot get through a year without leeks*

Next to onions they are the most important vegetable in the garden. They are best sown in April in a seedbed, or in March indoors in pots of compost. Leave the seedlings growing until they become pencil sized and in June they can be planted into their final positions. Cutting the roots and leaves is the best way and it doesn't really affect the growth of the plants, but it does give them time to bed in before they continue to grow.

I have taken to using a bulb planter these days. What I do now is trample the ground

COD and LEEK CASSEROLE

HAVE YOU EVER TRIED LEEKS WITH FISH?

CUT A POUND OF COD FILLET INTO PIECES

THEN WASH AND CUT UP 3 OR 4 NICE LEEKS

PUT A LAYER OF COD INTO A CASSEROLE, THEN A LAYER OF LEEK, SEASONING AS YOU GO

NOW POUR IN JUST ENOUGH HALF MILK AND HALF WATER TO COVER

PUT ON THE LID AND BAKE IN A MODERATE OVEN FOR ABOUT ½ HR.

THICKEN THE SAUCE AND POUR IT BACK TO SERVE THE FISH IN THE CASSEROLE— IT **ALWAYS** SAVES WASHING-UP!

using a plank, then cut out plugs of earth using the bulb planter and simply plonk a single leek into each hole. Then the holes are simply filled with water – there is nothing else to it. Within a month the leeks will be growing and the rain, or watering, will have made the holes

Harvest hints:
Tomatoes are renown for staying green when you want them red. Ripeness is controlled by a gas, ethylene, which is given off by the fruit itself.

This gas triggers the rest of the plant to manufacture other hormones that makes the fruit fall off, blow away, or change colour or otherwise attract animals to eat the fruit.

Very ripe fruit will induce ripening in tomatoes. Find yourself an unripe banana and hang it from a string near your tomatoes and within a day you will see the skin nearest the ripe fruit begin to turn red. Pears work even better than bananas, especially if you cut them in half.

The action of pulling a fruit off the branch induces the production of hormones, so the more you pick the riper the rest become.

Fertilizing the soil:
When you grow crops, much of what you take from the ground comes from the air and the soil. You need to replace the soil portion of what your crops have consumed and the best way to do this is old fashioned muck.

But you cannot use fresh muck, it is too strong. A cow's digestive system is designed to dissolve plants and it will carry on doing so until the muck has rotted. Pile your muck, cow is probably best and easiest to use, like a compost heap and cover with a tarpaulin. Leave this for a year and you will have some brilliant fertilizer.

fill with earth. When the plants have grown, by the end of August, you can draw soil around the leeks so that the stems are blanched.

Harvest by digging them out with a fork because they might snap if you simply pull them out.

Modern varieties include:

Apollo – *good disease resistance*
Musselburgh – *an old favourite*
Titan – *as its name suggests, huge!*

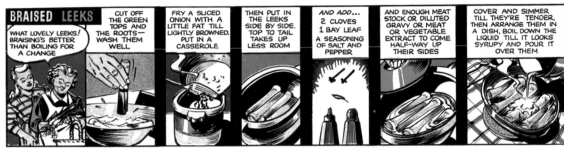

Fertilizing the soil:

Dig the soil in the winter as soon as the weather allows and then pile the muck, a forkful per metre square, and spread it out.

Leave it on the top and the worms in the soil will drag a lot of it in to the soil. A month before you are ready to plant, turn it over lightly with a fork, incorporating the manure into the soil.

Lettuce - *Lettuce is probably the most common salad nowadays*

You can eat lettuces all year round by constant sowing from December in the greenhouse to August in the bed. They prefer moist soil that is free draining, so there are no puddles.

LAMB'S LETTUCE

ORDINARY LETTUCE CAN BE DULL—STILL YOU'VE GOT TO HAVE IT FOR SALADS, I SUPPOSE

YOU DON'T **HAVE** TO. TRY **LAMB'S LETTUCE** OR, AS SOME SAY, **CORN SALAD**

IT'LL BE READY BY LATE SPRING, BUT SOW **NOW** IN SHALLOW DRILLS 6 INS. APART

IF YOU CAN START IT OFF UNDER TENT CLOCHES SO MUCH THE BETTER

THEY'LL NEED THINNING OUT TO 6 INS. APART

SOW OUTDOORS IN AUG. SEPT. FOR EARLY SPRING PICKING

IT'LL GROW TO 8 INS. HIGH. YOU PICK IT LIKE SPINACH, OUTSIDE LEAVES FIRST

IT'S TASTY ON ITS OWN AS A FRENCH-DRESSED SALAD — THAT'S WITH OIL AND VINEGAR

AND **VERY** GOOD WITH CELERY AND BEETROOT—WE CHEFS CALL IT **SALADE LORETTE**!

Transplanting lettuces

Lettuces do not like to be transplanted. It is because they have so much leaf, so unless you are going to transplant them as seedlings, they will have to be sown where they will grow.

Mark a drill in the soil that is about 1in (2cm) deep and use the finger and thumb to sow thinly. As they grow thin them out to about 3in (8cm) and then again to 6in (18cm).

Keep them moist but not wet and look out for slugs and greenfly. A regular sowing every fortnight until June will provide a crop through the whole summer and into the autumn.

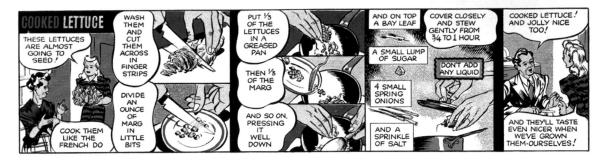

Varieties include:

Iceberg Great Lakes 659 – *a variety that does not go to seed, and is easy to grow*
Web – *a nice one for thick leaves and you can pull a single leaf off and leave the plant in the ground if you like*

Rocket

This is one of those plants that you can sow in the early spring and every fortnight until the end of September and get salad leaves for weeks into the winter. You can even sow them in October indoors and get some leaves in February in a cool but frost-free greenhouse or tunnel. The peppery taste, along with the wonderfully shaped leaves, makes a great addition to the salad bowl.

Sowing

Sow in drills, only one at a time, every two weeks, at the rate of about 1½–2in (4cm) apart. The seedlings germinate in a couple of weeks, depending on the weather. Water them well in and give them a little feed once a fortnight. The second row should be around 16in (40cm) from the first, and by the time you are sowing your third row you should be thinning out the first to a plant every 4–5in (10–12cm). Don't forget the mantra: use your thinnings!

Rocket needs little care, save perhaps protecting from flea beetle in the height of the summer (I cover with fleece) and keeping moist.

Nasturtium

A plant with a scientific name like *Tropaeolum* makes you think of the tropics. This hot plant actually comes from South America and is well worth looking after. It grows over everything and dies away in the winter if not cared for.

The big peppery leaves and gorgeous hothouse flowers are edible and make for a brilliant salad. The buds and fruits make excellent caper substitutes, pickled in vinegar. Monet, in his French garden at Giverny, famously allowed them to grow over the paths. He painted them many times, but ate them more!

You should sow nasturtium between May and June in well-weeded soil that is in full sun. One trick is to sow them in a pot, which you bury in the soil, then in September bring them into the greenhouse so that you can eat them through the winter. Also you can take cuttings in August that will take in the polytunnel and be ready to plant outdoors again in late spring.

The seeds need to be planted at random, two or three almost anywhere in the garden, for extra colour and an edible pretty crop.

You can harvest the leaves as and when you need them.

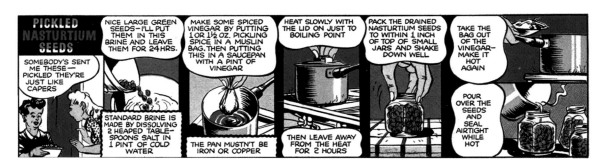

Mizuna

Mizuna is a brilliant salad. Grow it in well-drained soil, or containers, and you will be cropping for weeks. It's great raw in salads having a mild mustard taste. Mizuna is a robust plant that grows 10in (25cm) tall. You can cut it and it will grow again. It won't last the winter out, but you can grow it in pots and bring them into the greenhouse.

Sow in well-draining soil, in the sun, just like lettuce, and thin in the same way. You can do early sowings in March in modules indoors and transplant when the frost has finally cleared.

The plant can be harvested after three weeks and you simply use it on a cut-and-come-again basis.

Seed bed:

This is an area of soil in which seeds are sown to be transplanted to a final growing position. The most important thing is the soil is very finely crumbly, well drained and warm. It doesn't have to be particularly fertile soil because the seeds will grow with just water.

The soil has to be light and fluffy and you get to this stage by first digging it over, turning it with a fork and finally chopping for ages with a hoe. When this has finished, draw it to a smooth surface with a good quality rake.

Easy grow salads

It doesn't matter how much room you have, there's always space enough for a few salads. You can grow them in anything from an old teapot to a grow bag. You can grow them on a balcony (just remember to make sure they cannot blow away!) or you can grow them in a hanging basket. Even the windowsill is enough room!

Perhaps the most important thing to remember when you grow salads in containers is that for the most part they are leafy. Lettuces have a lot more leaf about them than root, as do all the beets, rockets, dandelions and so on.

Extra leaf means extra evaporation, and container grown salads lose water more than any other plant. They can dry out in a few hours on a dry day. Because of this they have to be watered more frequently – every day in the summer, even if it is raining!

When you water a container grown plant all the nutrients are washed away, leaving the compost or soil quite barren, so the container grown plant needs to be fed with liquid fertilizer once every other watering.

Onions

You should have onions on the go more or less all the time in the garden. They are fairly easy to grow as long as you keep them more or less weed-free and well-watered in well-draining soil.

Onions are biennials, which means they grow bulbs one year, flowers the next. Seed sown in December will be ready in summer. We used to say 'Sow on the shortest day of the year and harvest on the longest', but it's not quite that simple.

Sowing in trays is an easy job, thinning them out is harder. The best tip I can give you is HANDLE THE LEAF, NEVER THE STEM. Then everything will be easy. Simply make a hole in the compost with a pencil and then use the pencil to lever the onion seedling out of the tray into its new home.

Onion sets are manufactured. They have been specially treated to kill the flower bud inside the bulb leaving the plant no alternative other than to grow more bulb. You buy an onion weighing an ounce and get one weighing a

Have a go at old varieties:
Do you remember when they tried to ban King Edward potatoes? There was an outcry! How dare the European government try to tell us what to grow.

However, there are lots of varieties out there in just as much danger because we simply can't be bothered to grow them at all. We seem to buy just the ones the catalogues tell us.

There are a number of specialist heritage seed suppliers that provide plants that are just as good now as they were a hundred years ago.

For example, I remember the days when peas were six foot high. Most young 'uns probably think peas are only two feet high! Well grow some Shirley's Giant Exhibition and you'll soon see what a real pea is all about.

pound by the time the summer arrives. Use a dibber to make a small hole and push the set into it. Firm it in and a couple of weeks later check to see that the set hasn't thrown itself out of the soil.

Japanese onions are sown in their bed in June and over-wintered to be harvested in spring. They make good firm onions but they don't store as

MACARONI and ONION FRITTERS

OH DEAR! NO MEAT OR FISH! NOW LET'S SEE...

COOK 2 OZ. MACARONI AND CUT IT INTO SMALL PIECES

CHOP UP 4 OZ BOILED ONIONS

AND MIX WITH 3 OZ. BREADCRUMBS, SALT, PEPPER, AND A LITTLE PARSLEY IF YOU LIKE

ADD 2 RECONSTITUTED DRIED EGGS

SHAPE INTO SMALL ROUND FLAT CAKES

AND FRY BROWN ON EACH SIDE

WISH I'D GOT SOME TOMATO SAUCE! GRAVY'LL HAVE TO DO INSTEAD

well as main
crop summer onions. They
are ideal for an
early spring crop.

Cooking onions

Patsy had a lot of onion
recipes, but more than any
other vegetable, the flavour
comes from the garden
not the kitchen. Make sure
your onions are well fed
and disease free. More than
anything else, time spent
drying them after harvest
will reward the cook with
tasty food.

Spring Onions

These should be sown where they are to be harvested from April and every two weeks until mid-June. This will give an almost constant crop from the end of May until September. You can even plant them in pots and bring them into a cool greenhouse at the end of September. Thin them to about a hand's width once the plants are a few inches high and feed them every three weeks with liquid fertilizer.

I knew an old chap who had two permanent onion beds. He used to light bonfires on them before planting and grew his crop in the ashes. He never rotated his onions, but boy, he had some beauties!

Modern varieties include:

Sturon – *an old favourite and if you buy sets this is more or less all you can get*
Ailsa Craig – *big, beautiful onions mainly for exhibition*
Red Baron – *a red onion, very tasty*
Lisbon – *a salad onion type*
Express Yellow – *a Japanese onion*

Parsnips

These plants remain in the ground for longer than any other vegetable. They need to be sown in March at the latest to make a crop the following December and January. The old-fashioned way of sowing these plants in a hole in the ground filled with compost is still the best. The key with parsnips is to use fresh seed, warm the soil before sowing and a light covering of old potting compost to mark where they are. They need a lot of feed to make that wonderful aromatic flavour, so it's best to feed them monthly with liquid fertilizer.

Canker comes from a fungal infection that follows carrot fly attack or bad hoeing where you have just nicked the skin. You have to treat them with kid gloves, and protect them from carrot fly.

Parsnip flavour improves as the cold nights come in and a bit of frost is good for them. When you come to harvest parsnips, try to pick a day after a week of sunny weather. But harvesting is difficult if you are not going to snap the roots. Dig a deep hole next to the last plant and then use a fork to lift out the plant from the side.

COD and PARSNIPS

I ALWAYS LIKE A PARSNIP BUT HAVE YOU TRIED THEM WITH COD?

COOK A POUND OF COD FILLET AND FLAKE IT UP

KEEP IT HOT TILL WANTED

MEANWHILE PEEL AND COOK TWO PARSNIPS IN SLIGHTLY SALTED WATER TILL THEY'RE SOFT-RUB THROUGH A SIEVE

PUT THIS PURÉE INTO A SAUCEPAN WITH A LITTLE MILK AND WHEN ITS NICE AND SMOOTH AND HOT POUR IT OVER THE FISH

IF THAT'S A BIT TOO PARSNIPY FOR YOU JUST MAKE A WHITE SAUCE...

½ OZ. MARG
½ OZ. FLOUR
½ PT. MILK
AND
WATER THE FISH WAS COOKED IN

AND WHEN IT'S READY SIMPLY ADD A COOKED PARSNIP CUT IN SMALL DICE

I LIKE COLD PARSNIP WITH SALAD DRESSING TOO!

Modern varieties include:

Avonresister – *canker resistant to a degree*
White Gem – *a good old variety*
Panache – *a good new variety*
Archer – *one that will give you no problems*

Mulch:
Cover the soil around the plants with something that will cut down evaporation.

This can be plastic, compost, bark chippings, leaves, old carpet, anything that cuts down water loss.

It will also keep weeds down, another way of cutting down water loss.

Peas

Peas are a huge favourite in the garden. They have been ever since they were introduced in the sixteenth century. At one time it was complained that the workers in the fields were eating more peas than they collected. For nearly two hundred years the whole country was pea mad. They are still a basic staple on everyone's plate and there are so many local recipes for them.

When I first started growing peas the varieties were tall. As more farmers began harvesting peas with combine harvesters, the height of the common pea varieties became smaller to accommodate the needs of the machinery. Now most peas are dwarf in habit and

it is something special to see a large variety.

You can start peas off from March to July to get a succession of crops from late June until October. Planting them in August is always disappointing because there are no insects around to pollinate the flowers. We used to plant them in the drill and leave them to grow. If the mice didn't get them the pigeons would. However you can plant them in modules, small pots, newspaper pots, even gutters. Actually that's my favourite trick, to grow peas in gutters and transplant them by sliding them out into a drill.

Modern varieties include:

Kelvedon Wonder – *a great variety that can be started earlier*

Onward – *a good all rounder suitable for later sowing*

Peppers - *How little we understood peppers in the past!*

One of the first cultivated crops in the Americas was the chilli, grown over 9,000 years ago, and sweet peppers are really just one of the same family.

I don't grow them under cloches any more, but in a greenhouse, almost like a tomato. That way you get more consistent results. The best time to sow pepper seeds is mid-February through to mid-March, though you can leave it until later if you want. Just remember that some varieties can take a month or more to germinate.

Sow in good multipurpose compost and always use fresh stuff, never compost that has been used for something else. The soil needs to be around 21°C for germination, or even hotter. If you can, start peppers off in trays in a heated propagator. Once the first leaves have set the plants can be potted on. This can be left until the second leaves have set but don't leave it much later than that. You should pot up in stages first into a 3in pot then into a 6in and finally into a 10in or bigger depending on variety. Just like tomatoes!

Once the plants set flowers and start to fruit you can feed them with tomato fertilizer once a week. Don't over water and keep a watering can full of water inside the greenhouse to reach the same temperature as the air so that you don't cool the roots too much.

Testing the soil:
A soil test kit can tell you a lot. For a start you will know if your soil is acid or alkaline. This is important because the amount of acid controls how a plant takes in nutrients.

Most plants like a neutral or slightly alkaline soil. A general application of lime helps cabbages grow well. However potatoes hate lime, so plan accordingly.

You can test also for the amount of nutrients there are in the soil and then plan a regime of fertilizing the soil. In general, the darker the soil the more fertile it is.

A healthy soil grows a lot of weeds and the rule of thumb is if there are no weeds the soil is poor. If there are a lot of weeds it might look messy, but it is certainly fertile.

Potatoes - *Where would we be without potatoes?*

You get an amazing yield of potatoes compared with grain, enough to feed a family from an average garden. But they take care and a little knowledge.

Early potatoes need to be in the ground by mid-March – traditionally St Patrick's Day. It always fills me with excitement, planting potatoes. Anyone who has not experienced this is missing out on one of the greatest joys of life and anyone can do it, you don't even need soil!

There are two types of potato, waxy and floury. Floury potatoes are fluffy, used for roasting and making chips, or mashing. Waxy ones are best for boiling and making salads. The waxy potatoes have cell walls that do not burst whereas the floury potatoes explode inside on cooking.

In the UK, waxy potatoes include Nadine, Pink Fir Apple, Cara, Marfona, Home Guard and Sharp's Express; general purpose potatoes include Estima, Wilja, Saxon, Nicola, Charlotte, Kestrel, Maris Peer, Maris Piper, Romano and Désirée; and floury include King Edward, Sante and Golden Wonder.

VERY EARLY POTATOES

WHY NOT GROW REALLY EARLY POTATOES TO EAT WITH YOUR MINT?

MAY QUEEN ARE BEST IF YOU CAN GET THEM, OTHERWISE DUKE OF YORK

NOW OR NEXT MONTH PUT BROKEN CROCKS IN THE BOTTOM OF A 10-INCH POT, AND HALF FILL WITH JOHN INNES POTTING COMPOST NO. 1

PUT IN ONE SEED POTATO, EYE-END UPWARDS

AND COVER WITH ENOUGH OF THE COMPOST TO FILL TWO-THIRDS OF THE POT

PUT IT IN A FROST-PROOF GREENHOUSE OR CONSERVATORY– AND AS THE HAULM GROWS, WATER IN DOSES OF A GENERAL FERTILISER

NOW AND THEN TOP-DRESS WITH THE COMPOST TO KEEP THE TUBERS COVERED

ABOUT THE MIDDLE OF MAY WITH LUCK YOU SHOULD GET A COUPLE OF POUNDS OF SPUDS OFF YOUR ORIGINAL POTATO

ANYWAY IT'S WORTH TRYING–JUST TO BOAST ABOUT!

Growing times

The time needed for the plant to produce a reasonable crop is important. 'First Earlies' need around 12–15 weeks, depending on where you are in the country. 'Second Earlies' need 17–20 weeks and 'Maincrop' need 20–25 weeks.

Varieties:

First Early: *Maris Peer, Home Guard, Arran Pilot, Pentland Javelin, Rocket, Pink Fir Apple*

Second Early: *Kestrel, Wilja, Estima, Osprey, Nadine Maincrop varieties: Admiral, Cara, Eden, Maris Piper, King Edward*

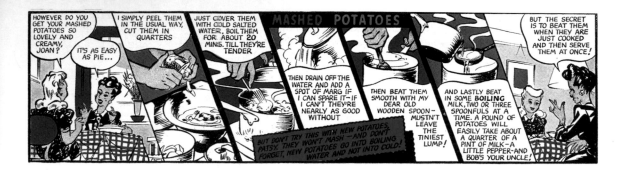

The soil

This must be well dug during the previous autumn and a lot of well-rotted manure should be added. This fills the soil with nutrients and makes it spongy since the potatoes absorb a lot of water. Always use fresh seed potatoes that are bought new each winter so that you do not carry on disease from last year.

Chitting potatoes

Simply leave your tubers in a light, airy, frost free place where they can acclimatize to their surroundings. Enzymes inside the potato start to convert starch to sugar and as soon as the buds get sugar they burst into life. The potato becomes soft as the starch is used up and then the potato is ready for planting.

Planting

Dig a trench 1 spade deep by 1 spade wide and about 25ft (10m) long. Simply lay your potatoes with the buds (also known as eyes) uppermost and cover with soil. Earlies should be spaced at 18in (45cm) apart, maincrop potatoes should be spaced at 2ft 6in (75cm) apart. The rows should be 2ft 6in (75cm) apart, perhaps a little narrower for earlies.

Care of your potatoes

They need plenty of water, but water at soil level and only in dry periods, never on the plants (now called vines) themselves. As they grow, pull up soil around the plants, a process known as 'earthing up'. This will protect the tubers from going green. Watch out for blight, a topic we deal with fully in a later chapter.

Family

Potatoes are part of the same family as tomatoes. This is an interesting fact, especially when you see the fruits appearing on the potato vines. Don't eat them though, because they are so full of alkaloids you'll get an amazing tummy ache, and you will stop absorbing important vitamins. You must be careful not to transfer disease from the potato patch to the tomatoes. Both suffer from blight, so be very careful.

Cooking

Potatoes need to be very well cooked. Otherwise they can give you an upset tummy, and if you were to eat four large raw potatoes you would become very ill indeed. Always make

sure you do not eat green potatoes at any time and always store them in a dark place. It is interesting that the other famous member of the potato family is deadly nightshade.

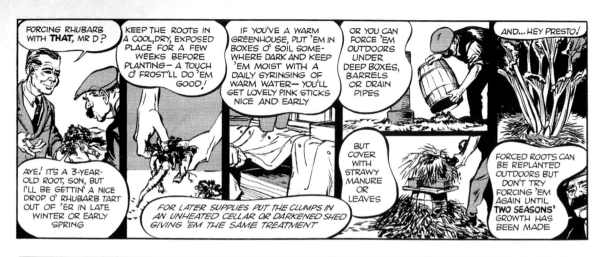

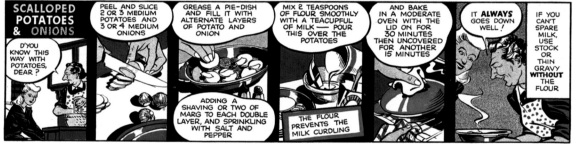

Rhubarb - *This is the funniest plant, a vegetable that we eat for pudding; there aren't many of those*

Since they come from Siberia they are very frost hardy, in fact a harsh frost does them good – you get a better flavour.

You normally buy rhubarb as crowns, which are basically roots with a little bit of rhizome on the top. In October, dig a good sized (2ft or 60cm square) hole and fill it with a mixture of rich compost, soil and well-rotted manure in equal volumes. Leave this for a few weeks for the soil to settle and then in November plant the crown in this. Bury it the right way up, but you don't need to see it. Firm it in well and mulch with a layer of compost.

By spring you will have the first shoots. Leave them to grow this year, mulching with more compost in spring, not touching the plant. Water as necessary. When the leaves die back in autumn, mulch yet again – keep this regime going all the time. The following spring you will have wonderful stalks to pull off.

What's that disease?
It is important to recognize different sources of disease so you can decide what is the next step.

Fungal problems:
If there is a smell, sliminess, powder on leaves, black splodges on leaves, it is likely to be fungal in origin.

This can be treated by spraying with copper fungicide, increasing the ventilation, reducing the temperature, simply cutting off the infection and burning the plant.

Best avoided by not growing in too humid conditions.

Varieties:

I have grown Canada Red, Riverside Giant (which is green) and of course, Timperly Early, which I think is the best because it never fails to produce a brilliant crop.

Salsify

This interesting plant is sown as I said way back in a rich bed. They are also known as oyster plant because they taste a little like seafood. They grow very happily in a trench or a bed and look like little clumps of grass. Scorzonera is a similar vegetable known as Black Salsify and grows in the same way.

Sow in March and water in. You will be surprised by the seedlings which look a little like small twigs popping out of the soil. They take a long time to harvest, but you will have roots available by the end of September and they will benefit from a good liquid feed once or twice in the summer.

Cooking salsify is a bit troublesome. You need to peel the roots, and they bleed over your fingers. Pop them into water with a little lemon juice and then chop the root into small pieces if you are going to boil them. There are lots of recipes for oyster plant mash too.

Seakale

This is a brassica, like cabbage or sprouts, so you have to avoid putting it in ground infected with clubroot. Otherwise it is an easy crop that is tolerant of low nutrients and low water.

Seeds can take up to three years to germinate, so don't bother. Instead, buy the roots from the nursery or garden centre and plant as shown. Leave them in any old corner of the plot so long as it is fairly bright. In their first year leave them to grow without taking a crop, but in their second year take some of the shoots as you would asparagus. In the second

SEAKALE

THE POOR MAN'S ASPARAGUS!

WELL, GET THEM ROOT-CUTTINGS IN SHARPISH, MATE! DON'T FORCE 'EM MIND...LET 'EM GROW NATURALLY IN DEEP-DUG SOIL WITH PLENTY O' COMPOST IN THE TWO BOTTOM SPITS...SEAWEED'S IDEAL

THE ROOTS ARE USUALLY CUT SO...

PLANT, SLANT END DOWN, IN ROWS 2½ FEET APART, THE TOPS 2 INCHES BELOW GROUND LEVEL

PUT A 9 INCH HEAP OF LEAVES OVER EACH CROWN WITH A SPRINKLE OF EARTH ON TOP

OR HEAPS OF SOIL ONLY'LL DO, IF IT'S SANDY OR SIEVED WITH ASHES, ELSE YOU'LL HAVE IT STICKIN' TO THE GROWTHS

WHEN THE SHOOTS SHOW THROUGH, CUT 'EM OFF CLEAN WITH A BIT OF THE ROOT ATTACHED

THEY NEED 20 MIN. BOILING OR STEAMING FOR AN HOUR—SERVE WITH BUTTER AND LEMON JUICE OR COLD IN SALAD...

year you can take two-thirds of them. Leave the rest to grow.

Seakale is a perennial plant so it will come again each year. All you need to do is give it a good dressing of compost in the spring and a feed once or twice in the watering in the summer. Apart from this, the plant will lose its vigour after about seven years, and so you should remove old plants replacing with new. You can make new plant by taking four-year-old seakale and dividing the roots to give you fresh stock, so once you have a stock going you shouldn't run out.

Bacterial problems:
Because the cell walls of plants are hard and cold, bacterial infections are not so common. However, some black spots on leaves and rotting stems are bacterial in origin. They do not respond to treatment, the plant should be burned.

Viral problems:
Discoloured leaves, strange lumps and warts are caused by viral infections which have no cure really other than cutting the infected part and burning. You might find the rest of the plant is OK, but frequently it is best to remove the whole plant than risking the health of the rest of the crop.

Sweetcorn

Prolonged hot summers are excellent for sweetcorn. This is a good crop to grow because it is relatively undemanding, especially regarding soil type, and suffers few pest and disease problems. Modern varieties have been bred to be more tolerant of our climate conditions and there are many types to choose from.

These days we tend to grow sweetcorn in a square grid because this improves the germination. Sweetcorn is essentially a tall stout grass, and, being wind pollinated, if you grow it in a straight line it is less likely to be pollinated.

Dig the soil deeply, to around 2ft (60cm) in March and leave it to settle. If you can put black plastic on the patch this is even better.

In April, in a heated greenhouse, sow two seeds to a 3in (8cm) pot and discard the slowest grower. Water these and keep them indoors until late May, even early June. Simply plant them out into a square grid. The least number of plants you should have is nine to make three short rows of three plants each, spaced at around 2ft (60cm) intervals.

Apart from this there is little to do to them except water and maybe a weekly feed of liquid fertilizer while the heads are pollinating and filling out. It's sunshine they need more than anything else.

Modern varieties include:

Aztec – *good one for cold climates*
Lark FI – *a very sweet variety that needs more sun*
Strawberry – *a miniature variety – great fun*

Swede

This vegetable is unusual because, being a brassica you would have thought it would be sown in early spring, but it's a couple of months later than that. Neither is it related to the turnip, which for some reason people mistake it for.

As with all aromatic flavoured plants it needs a lot of nutrients, so dig in a lot of well-rotted manure and work the soil until you have a fine tilth. The seeds take about a couple

of weeks to germinate, and then you start to thin them out. The thinnings are great in salads – they have a peppery flavour and are quite nutritious.

You could start pulling swedes from September if you wanted to, but they are much

better if you pull them out of the ground in December or January, once the frost has got at them. There really is no need to pull them for storage because they keep well in the soil.

Being brassicas they can get clubroot, so I like to incorporate a lot of lime into the soil to keep this at bay. You can also grow them in pots and transplant them like cabbages, but I have never tried that method, as they are not as susceptible to disease as other brassicas.

Tomatoes

There is nothing more gratifying than cutting into that first tomato that you have grown yourself. If you think of summertime it simply has to include tomatoes. But today there are even more reasons for growing tomatoes – tended in your own garden, they are non-polluting, cheap, cheerful and taste great!

Start sowing in March

If you have an unheated greenhouse or polytunnel, mid-March to early-April is the best time to start sowing your tomatoes. Use good quality compost and sow your plants either in modules, seed trays or 3in (8cm) pots. I use those foam plastic drinks cups and place two or

three seeds per pot, pricking out the weakest plants once they have a couple of leaves on them and I can judge which one is best to keep.

Place the trays or pots in a heated propagator (20°C/68°F) and germination should take about a week. Once the young plants have reached a handbreadth height, they can be moved to a sunny spot for a week or so to acclimatize them to their final growing place.

We used to transplant tomatoes from small pots through larger ones until they ended up in a 10in (25cm) pot or ring culture pot. This tends not to be the way we grow them nowadays.

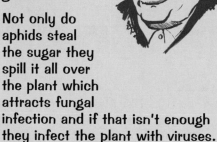

Killing Aphids:
Early summer brings the most voracious pest in the garden.

Not only do aphids steal the sugar they spill it all over the plant which attracts fungal infection and if that isn't enough they infect the plant with viruses.

Killing aphids is easy enough but you have to be on the ball all the time. Just a few days of respite will see them coming back with a vengeance. Greenfly and blackfly can be killed in many ways.

Finger and thumb:
My favourite way is to simply squash them, but this cannot be done on delicate plants because you will damage them. However, it is possible to keep them down to a reasonable number.

Planting out

Once the plants are big enough to handle – usually from mid-May – you can transplant them into their growing position. If you have a tunnel or large greenhouse, put them in a rich bed – either straight in the ground, or use ring culture pots, which have no bottoms but allow you to water the growing plant more easily. You push them in the soil, fill with compost and plant your tomato inside. I also use them for cucumbers.

The benefit of this is that you just water inside the pot and don't increase the humidity of the greenhouse or polytunnel by pouring water willy-nilly around the soil.

The plants should be 16in (40cm) apart, and supported right from day one. I use garden canes – big ones, firmed deep in the compost. I have also used a series of strings from the top of the greenhouse, but find them to be too harsh when the plant gets heavy.

Growbags are also acceptable, but be careful not to buy the cheap ones because the compost isn't brilliant. And only put two plants per bag, not three as they seem to suggest. Water the plants well, keeping the soil slightly moist – but do not over water. Too much water at the early stage can promote fungal infections. After a few weeks you will be amazed by the first truss. This is a flowering branch – and once you see this, get watering and feeding. If the weather is hot, water carefully every day – don't splash it about! Once a week add some tomato fertilizer to the watering.

Soft Soap:
A high powered jet of soap solution will knock them off the plant and kill them by dehydration. The soap dissolves the wax on their bodies and they simply dry out.

Chemicals:
I try not to use chemicals but if you have a bad infestation then buy one of the organic hand sprays that will clear them out in a few hours.

Biological Control:
Both ladybirds and lacewings eat hundreds of aphids each day in the garden and you can buy them as larvae or adults. This form of control is best in the greenhouse where the prey insects cannot fly away.

GREEN TOMATOES

GOSH! I'LL NEVER RIPEN ALL THESE!

AH! EASIEST WAY'S TO REMOVE THE STAKES AND LAY THE **PLANTS** DOWN ON DRY PEAT OR CUT-UP STRAW

COVER WITH WELL-VENTILATED CLOCHES

BUT KEEP THE GLASS CLEAN—THEY'LL WANT ALL THE LIGHT POSSIBLE

IF YOU'VE A GREENHOUSE, LAY THE FRUIT ON DRY STRAW ON THE STAGING—(**NOT** TOUCHING,!)

OR HANG THE WHOLE TRUSSES IN A WARM, SUNNY PLACE

OF COURSE, THERE'S THE OLD DODGE OF STORING THEM IN A DRAWER WRAPPED IN TISSUE PAPER OR NEWSPAPER

BUT SEE THAT THE DRAWER'S **NOT** AIR-TIGHT, AND LOOK 'EM OVER CAREFULLY NOW AND THEN

Side shoots

The plant will produce shoots – branches that come from the leaf nodes of the main vine. Cut these out – mostly because the plant will grow like a bush, increasing the humidity in the greenhouse.

Keep supporting the plants as they grow by loosely tying them to the cane or support. You will have to decide how many trusses you want from your plants. Three per plant gives bigger tomatoes but you will not get maximum yield. Four or five is the norm, but you can get as many as seven or eight if you have room to grow such a tall plant. The way to control the number of trusses is to pinch out the topmost growing point.

Harvesting

Ripening of tomatoes is controlled by a gaseous plant hormone – ethylene. This gas is given off by ripe fruit and triggers the ripening process. This is why you sometimes see a ripe banana hanging inside a greenhouse.

Of course, late August to late September is the major harvest time for tomatoes. You just can't eat them all! But there is nothing better than being able to bottle or chutney or dry them. This way your crop will last the whole year through.

Outdoor tomatoes

In some years the outdoor tomatoes do better than the indoor ones. In May plant those destined for outdoor life into 12in (30cm) pots but keep them inside until the end of June. Thereafter put them out during the day and back in at night for a week until they acclimatize to outdoor life.

Treat as though they were indoor tomatoes but only allow four trusses to develop as a maximum. This reduced yield is made up for by the fact that you can grow a lot more tomatoes outside than inside.

Container growing
Five tips for good container plants:

1. Use the biggest you can – the more compost you have the better for keeping nutrients available to your plant.

2. Water every day in summer – containers do not keep much water and you need to water daily, even if it has been raining.

3. Feed every week – if you are watering a lot, you wash away the nutrients so you have to replace them by feeding regularly.

Tomatoes came from south America where they grew used to high temperatures. It gained total prominence in the sixteenth century where it became known as the apple of love. Goodness knows why it got this name, but this is one of the reasons that it was considered dangerous to eat by religious people. It was many years before strains were developed that ripened red rather than yellow.

Today you can get all kinds of colours from red to yellow and even striped forms. It has become one of the most important vegetables in the world; whole cuisines are given up to its preparation. It is one of the healthiest vegetables a young boy can eat, especially when cooked. It is packed with lycopene which helps to protect him from male cancers in later life.

Tomatoes come in the following varieties or forms:

Standard – *the basic tomato we buy in the shops every day*
Cherry – *these are small ones that explode in the mouth when you bite them*
Steak – *enormous toms – a single slice covers a sandwich*
Plum – *mostly Italian, like the ones you get in tins*
Marmande – *large irregular shaped tomatoes, often very tasty*
Oxheart – *sort of heart shaped, pretty and tasty too*

4. Move the plants – you can move your pots so they enjoy the best of the sunlight, the best of the warmth near the house at night.

5. Use the best compost you can – do not grow plants in compost that is not fully ripe, you will simply rot your plants.

Don't just rely on the compost from a growbag, they are usually not that fertile.

Turnips

These are the easiest plants to grow in the world. It seems strange but you sow them just like the Japanese onions. Thin them out by removing every other plant. They tend to be at their best when they are just about the size of a cricket ball.

You can sow any time from April to September (use a cloche in September) and they will give you a great crop all the winter through. Turnips are easy to grow – just keep them on fairly well maintained soil, with plenty of organic material dug in. The only other thing they need is reasonable sun and not to ever actually dry out.

Turnips, unlike swedes, do not get very fibrous, and when roasted are extremely sweet. Once harvested, remove the tops and compost them because they are packed with nutrients and make an excellent compost.

SAVOURY TURNIPS

THESE SIX YOUNG TURNIPS WILL BE ENOUGH FOR US TWO – THE TOPS I'LL USE AS GREENS

PARE AND CUT UP THE TURNIPS IN THIN SLICES

PUT A LAYER IN THIS PIE-DISH. SPRINKLE WITH A LITTLE GRATED CHEESE, SALT, PEPPER AND NUTMEG

AND SO ON TILL THEY'RE FINISHED. THEN POUR IN A BREAKFASTCUP OF MILK OR GRAVY

SPRINKLE WITH BREADCRUMBS AND A LITTLE MELTED FAT

AND BAKE IN A MODERATE OVEN FOR ½ HOUR OR SO

I'LL COME WITH YOU AND THANK DAD – BUT I WON'T CADGE ANYTHING THIS TIME!

There are a number of problems you always have to be on the look out for:

- Too much water/too dry
- Not enough food
- Not enough sun/too cold/too warm
- Pests
- Too crowded/too many weeds
- Too acidic/too limey

Aftercare

Growing good crops is not just a case of plonking the plant in the ground and then leaving it to its own devices. There is much to do and you need to be constantly on your metal to keep up.

As a quick reference the table on the next pages gives you an at-a-glance picture of the vegetable year.

	Jan	Feb	Mar	Apr	May
Soil	Digging – Feeding.				
Plants	Purchasing – Sowing.			Sow – Plant – Protect from pests.	
General	Clean tools, greenhouse.			Maintain paths, beds.	
Potatoes	Feed & dig the potato patch.		Plant Earlies.		Plant in maincrop.
Turnips	Prepare soil, dig in compost.				
Swede	Dig but don't manure.				
Parsnip	Harvest from December.	Sow in spring, or even Febuary.			
Carrots	Prepare as parsnip.	Sow in February under cover, & in the open until June.			
Cabbage	Dig soil, add compost & lime.		Sow from mid-spring to summer in succession. Transplant to final position or thin to 2in (50cm).		
Broccoli	Make the soil crumbly & fertile. Add bonemeal.			Sow outside in May, covered in April.	
Peas	Dig well, do not add nitrogen.		Sow from March to June every month to give a succession of crop.		
Onions	Dig and add compost.		Plant sets (small bulbs). Protect from frost. Sow salad onions until June. Thin to 6in (15cm).		
Salads	Find spaces among your beds to continually sow lettuce, radish, chives, rocket, endive, & yes – have a go at dandelion (only never let them flower!).				

Jun	Jul	Aug	Sep	Oct	Nov	Dec
Weeding – Feeding – Watering.			Harvesting – Clearing – Resting.			
	Nurture – Watering & Feeding.		Harvesting – Storing.			Prune.
	Water supply.		Turn Compost.		Planning.	
	Harvest Earlies – Maincrop.			Plan rotation – Move the crop.		

Sow & harvest after two months. Keep a supply going by sowing right into the end of August. Thin to 6in (18cm).

In the north sow in spring; in the south sow in midsummer. Thin to 18in (50cm).

Harvest as they are ready until frost.

Parsnips need no real care, sow them in drills (a scrape of earth & cover with soil) & thin to 8in (20cm).

Thin to 6in (15cm) & harvest from June to September.

Harvest from summer onwards.
Winter cabbages can be sown in September.

Harvest as florets appear.

Collect as pods fill sufficiently.

Collect salad onions, harvest others when leaves fall over & yellow.

Sow winter onions outside.

Delicious Fruit in the Garden

Every year the gardening catalogues arrive, usually in November, and they are packed with ideas for new fruit and vegetables. At one time new plants were produced by dedicated men in greenhouses who patiently crossed one plant with another to see what would emerge. They would then test their plants to see if they were in any way better. These days the process is much more science than art and we have a whole new range of plants to grow.

F1 Hybrid plants and modern fruit varieties

Years ago there was no such thing as F1 Hybrid plants in the shops. They are crosses of two plants that are always more vigorous than either of their parents that made them. They usually have much improved disease resistance and sometimes produce bigger crops too. F1 flowers are either different – have a double flower rather than a single, or have unusual markings or colours. I remember everyone was trying to make a perfectly black flower at one time – I'm glad they stopped!

Often F1 hybrid plants are completely sterile, or produce seeds that are sterile. Mostly, however, F1 hybrids do not breed true. You could not keep the seeds for next year, sow them and expect them to come true. A proportion of them will be like the parents, the rest will revert to how the plants that made the F1 Hybrid looked. And they will have their characteristics when it comes to disease resistance.

The only way to be continually happy with F1 plants is to buy new ones each season, which is sensible when it comes to all your seeds too really.

Why do we need new varieties?

Anyone who has grown plants year after year, plants like strawberries for instance, will know that they 'go off'. In fact, you should remove any strawberry plants that are three years old because they become increasingly susceptible to viral diseases. As time goes on, all the plants of that type that stock in your garden become weakened because of disease and what was once a good cropper slowly becomes a bad one. And all round the country the same thing is happening, so that as a variety it slowly becomes less useful.

Then there is the issue of disease resistance. Potatoes are also prone to disease. Potato blight can be tackled with chemicals, or by using a disease-resistant strain like 'Cara'. The growing organic movement has demanded a lot of inbuilt disease resistance, and so many new varieties of blight-resistant tomatoes and mildew-resistant gooseberries have turned up over the years.

There are commercial reasons for bringing out new plants, too. Nurserymen like to produce bigger, better plants with more flavour. Then there is the desire people have for growing new crops from abroad. The kiwi has now become popular, for example. At one time you needed male and female plants and they grew into really huge plants. But the males were not very happy in our climate, and when the 'Jenny' variety came along, the need for males was done away with. Now most people can grow their own kiwi.

New fruits

So, for the reasons mentioned above, nurseries produce new varieties of plants all the time and will have to for ever. It's just the way nature influences gardeners and their products. Here are some current new varieties that will, in years to come, be replaced by something else.

Strawberries

Amelia – *a late season variety*
Lucy – *a mid-season variety, which produces excellent yields of large berries*
Sallybright – *crops slightly earlier in the season and produces very regular shaped berries, which have an excellent flavour*

ONCE ESTABLISHED, PLANTS NEED A GOOD WATER SUPPLY, THROUGH A 5 INCH POT SUNK NEARBY

Blackcurrants

Titania – *immune to various diseases including white pine blister rust and powdery mildew. You get large, good quality fruit and a very large yield.*

Redcurrants

Redpoll – *a new very late redcurrant. It's a heavy cropper and has some resistance to leaf spot.*

Gooseberry

Pax – *a mid-season, red-fruited gooseberry. Mature plants lose most of their thorns and there is some resistance to mildew.*

Raspberry

Glen Ample – *gives masses of fruit and was developed in Scotland so it should cope with everything the weather throws at it.*
Julia – *slightly smaller than most but packed with flavour.*
Gaia – *is resistant to many diseases, this one is sure to be a winner.*

Blackberries

Helen – *a thornless blackberry that is early maturing, before August.*

Passing fad?

A lot of plants that come into the garden these days are simply passing crazes and will not go very far. Do you remember those cabbages that looked just like flowers?

We all grew them for a year or two, but no one does these days. Plants like 'Goji berries', which come from the Himalayas, have recently become popular and have been bred for growing in our climate. There are dozens of them; they come and go. When you look at new varieties, try to choose ones that are like the old ones but propose to have disease resistance or a better flavour. Trial them yourself, alongside your old favourite, to see how it goes. There is no point throwing the baby out with the bathwater.

Apples and bare-rooted fruit trees

There is no such thing as dormancy in deciduous plants (plants that drop their leaves). People think these plants are asleep, so that we can do all sorts of jobs on them. The truth is that all plants are doing something all the time. In the case of deciduous plants they are storing, moving stores around and as the leaves come back they burst into growth. However, we are able to perform drastic operations on plants so long as they do not have any leaves. Once the leaves are gone from the plant it will not lose too much water if you cut into it. When the leaves return you should leave well alone.

Bare or ball?

Fruit trees come either as bare-rooted or ball-rooted specimens. Bare-rooted plants come in a plastic bag, ready pruned and it usually has wet newspaper around the roots. Ball-rooted plants come with a ball of roots in a net of compost. Ball-rooted trees are usually found in garden centres and are more convenient because they can be watered and the tree will manage for a year or so quite happily, provided it doesn't dry out.

You can plant ball-rooted plants at any time during the year but be careful with the roots, and give them plenty of water. You must only plant bare-rooted plants if they have no leaves on them, so mostly they are planted in winter.

Ball-rooted trees establish themselves more easily than bare-rooted ones because their roots are a little better at growing quickly.

Rootstocks

In order to ensure that apples are always the same variety, they are grown from cuttings on to a root. It was discovered that if you graft apple shoots on to different kinds of roots you end up with different sized trees. Dwarfing rootstocks produce tiny trees, semi-dwarfing produce slender trees about 10ft (3m) tall, and there are also free rootstocks. The label on the tree will give you all the information you need.

The graft can be seen as a round wound on the tree where the branch (also known as a scion) is joined to the root (also known as the stock).

How to plant

Put your plants in the ground as soon as you can. Dig a hole 3ft (1m) in diameter and 2ft (60cm) deep. Keep your soil and remove weed roots and stones as you go. I put the soil on a plastic sheet and mix in a few spadefuls of good quality compost. A handful of bone meal or

other organic fertilizer is a good additive – just remember to wear gloves.

When you are ready to plant, put a tree-stake into the centre of the hole and drive it home. People often do this once the tree has been planted and the hole filled, but this may damage the roots. Put some of your soil mixture in the bottom of the hole and then set the tree in place. Firmly fill the hole with the rest of the soil and make a mound. The wood should just be proud of the soil level. Tie the tree to the stake with a tree tie, not string.

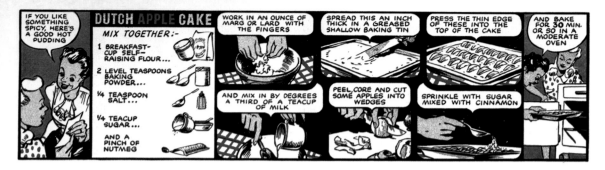

Give the tree a good drink of water after you have trodden it in. This forces the soil into contact with the roots. It can be up to three years before you get good quality fruit, and these early days are important. Feed the plant with good quality compost each spring, and keep it free from disease wherever possible. Make sure you weed the area near the tree and feed it with liquid fertilizer each month in the summer of its first year.

Apricots

Unlike peaches, apricots are easy to grow in this country as long as you have enough heat. Preferably you need to train the tree against a south-facing wall, but a greenhouse or polytunnel would be even better.

Apricots don't suffer from peach leaf curl, a disease that can cause severe leaf loss on plants grown outside. Their big problem is that the flowers appear early and can be damaged by frost, so you have to be ready to protect them. The tree grows very high and if you have it in a polytunnel you need a good 6ft (2m) headroom and you will probably grow it along the centre of the tunnel, along the path, trained along wires.

One tip, if you grow apricots in a tunnel or greenhouse: there probably aren't enough insects around to pollinate the flowers, so you will have to transfer pollen from one to another yourself. Do this with a soft brush – and be gentle. Apricots are self-fertile, so you need keep only one plant.

Modern varieties include:

Moor Park – *the most common*
Golden Glow – *a British variety*
Flavourcot – *ideal for the UK because it is not so dependent on heat*

Avocados

Growing avocado from a stone is fun – you never quite know what is going to happen. But then there are so many others you can try. Orange pips will give you a plant, and if you keep it warm, fed and watered, you will get flowers and possibly fruit.

When you buy fruits from the supermarket it is often a temptation to see if you could grow the thing for yourself, a bit like a house plant. You'd be amazed at what can be achieved with a little patience. I wouldn't bother with apple pips

Top fruit and soft fruit

" Top fruit are all those varieties that produce fruit above the level of your head; apples and pears, damsons, cherries – all these are called top fruit. Soft fruit are those varieties that produce a crop at or near the ground level. "

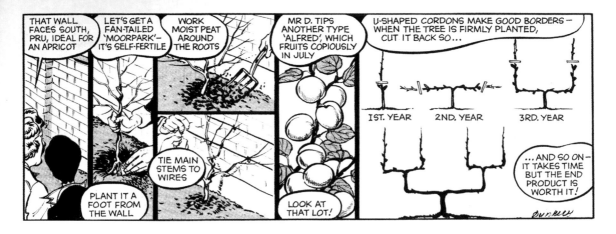

because we normally grow them on rootstocks and the tree will take years to get anywhere. An orange, on the other hand, is a must. As a general rule just pop the seeds in some moist compost and keep them warm and watered.

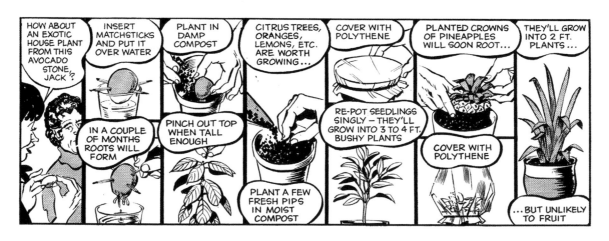

Pineapples

Yes! You can grow pineapples. During the Second World War, when you couldn't get them, we used to try all sorts of tricks to make them grow. This one was the most successful.

Twist the leaves off the top of the pineapple and eat the fruit. Pull away at the bottom leaves and you will find little rootlets which look as though they were maggots. Leave them on a windowsill for a few days to dry a little and then soak the whole thing in water. This sparks the roots into life and you should pot into an 8in (20cm) pot of compost. Don't let it get too wet, but water weekly. In the summer you can leave the plant outside but bring it indoors once the evenings cool. After a couple of years the plant will flower and then you should get a small fruit. Keep the plant well fed and pot on to a larger container.

Fast good. Slow bad. Many people do not know which insect and other mini beasts in the soil are good for the gardener and which are bad.

As a general rule the slow moving creatures are usually plant eaters while the fast moving ones are usually meat eaters.

They have to be fast moving in order to catch their prey. So if it moves quickly it's gardener's friend.

Actually even the slow moving ones aren't usually that much trouble because they often only eat damaged or decaying material.

But now you know which ones to throw on to next door's plot when you're digging.

Blackcurrants

You buy plants in October or November and dig a large hole into which you have incorporated plenty of well-rotted manure. Then plant the new blackcurrant into this. Prune each branch to two or three buds from the ground and then give it a good mulch with well-rotted compost.

When the weather is dry give it a good watering and during the following year you will get plant development at the expense of fruit. As I said, cut out any flowering branches once they have fruited. Give it another feed in autumn and mulch to protect it in the winter. From then on the care of the plant is easy.

You can make new plants by taking a shoot about 18in (45cm) long once the leaves have fallen off. Stand these in a nursery bed of moist compost in autumn and forget them until late next summer. Keep them weed free and then carefully dig them up in September or October to transplant to their final growing positions.

IF YOU WANT YOUR FULL QUOTA O' VITAMIN C NEXT YEAR, MR B, MIND HOW YOU PRUNE THEM **BLACK CURRANTS**... JUST C'MERE A JIFF

THE CURRANTS'LL FORM ON THE NEW SHOOTS PRODUCED DURING LAST SUMMER

SO CUT OUT THE OLD FRUITED BRANCHES AS LOW DOWN AS YOU CAN ON THE BUSH

BUT IF THE NEW SHOOTS ARE ON **SIDE-GROWTHS** FROM THE OLD BRANCHES, CUT EACH BRANCH BACK TO JUST ABOVE THE BEST SIDE-GROWTHS...

THIS'LL GIVE YOU A WELL-THINNED BUSH ALL READY FOR NEXT SUMMER'S CROP

... AND TALKIN' O' CURRANTS REMEMBER THIS... **RED** AND **WHITE** ONES BEAR FRUIT ON THEIR **OLD** WOOD, SO WHAT I'VE BEEN SAYIN' APPLIES TO **BLACK CURRANTS** ONLY!

DUNKLEY

Blackberries

Blackberries are easy-grow plants and can be found just as often in the wild as in gardens.
They need a sunny spot to make all that juice and try to incorporate a very large amount of
compost and well-rotted manure into the soil before planting. Make sure you buy disease-
free stock from the garden centre or nursery and try not to accept 'gifts' of blackberries from
well-intentioned gardeners.

They need to be planted in early spring in moist soil about 5ft (1.5m) apart and cut them

GOOSEBERRY PRUNING
I LIKE TO LEAVE PRUNING AS LATE IN JANUARY AS POSSIBLE TO DISCOURAGE BULLFINCHES EATING THE BUDS

THEY FIND IT MORE DIFFICULT TO PENETRATE A MASS OF PRICKLY SHOOTS LIKE THIS BUSH HAS

THIN OUT THE BRANCHES AND OPEN OUT THE CENTRE BY CUTTING BACK THE LOW-GROWING ONES TO AN UPWARD POINTING BUD OR SIDE SHOOT

TAKE OUT ANY CROSSING BRANCHES AND CUT BACK MAIN STEMS BY HALF, AND THE SIDE-SHOOTS TO 2 INCHES

IMMEDIATELY AFTER PRUNING, SPRAY WITH A COMMERCIAL TAR DISTILLATE BY MAKER'S INSTRUCTIONS, WHICH FURTHER DISCOURAGES THE BIRDS

BUT DON'T LEAVE THIS SPRAY LATER THAN THE END OF JANUARY OR IT MAY HARM THE BUDS

What not to compost:
It is a perfectly good idea to put your peelings and vegetables on the compost heap. They are already partially broken down and you can use the cooking water too.

However, don't ever compost gravy, meat, fish or anything straight from the plate. This is the quickest way to attract bluebottles and worse, rats, into the garden.

Once rats get to know your compost heap it is pretty difficult to get them out without demolishing the lot and starting again.

down to just 6in (15cm) which seems harsh, but they will be better for it. Each spring and autumn give them a good mulch of well-rotted manure.

Do not transfer blackberries from the wild into the garden. The wild varieties are usually riddled with viral infections and do not fruit quite so well. Blackberries are a most interesting plant because they hybridize so easily, and you get crosses of so many different types. You can get thornless blackberries, but I like to grow mine along a fence to act as a barrier to other people's pets – keeping them out of the garden. You have to be fastidious with pruning and shaping them, otherwise you will be left with a huge matted mess of canes you can't penetrate.

Raised Beds:
There are lots of good reasons for making raised beds. They drain more easily, you can deal with weeds more easily and it certainly keeps you off the soil.

Raised beds can be made from anything; wood, bricks, concrete slabs or plastic.

Gooseberries

If all you have is a north-facing wall the gooseberry is an ideal plant because it is quite happy with its teeth in a howling gale, and when the weather gets hot it starts to build up fruit at lightning speed. The only problem is that the fruit takes a few days to sweeten after a hot spell, so don't pick them on hot sunny days – leave them a bit longer and take advantage of the extra sugar rush.

Because of their good root system, gooseberries do well in poor soil just so long as they are well drained because they don't like to be too wet. Plant them from October until January. Plant in the same way as you do any fruit tree, add a little grit to the bottom of the hole to improve drainage.

Firm the plant in well with your heel and give it a mulch of compost on the top.

Always remember that the mulch should never actually touch the stem of the plant which will rot if the compost gets wet. Plant gooseberries at 5ft (1.5m) spaces and leave them to bed in.

Each spring mulch the plant and again in the autumn. A handful of slow release fertilizer will also do them good.

Pruning in February is simple: all you are looking to do is make an open plant with no crossing twigs and has plenty of air circulating around the fruits when they finally appear.

Grapevines - *A reputation for being difficult*

But not so! Grapes grow best in areas where the spring is dry, the summer is hot and the winter is cold. That can be the British climate to a 'T'. Just remember...

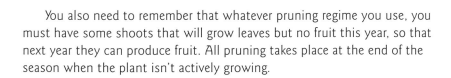

It takes a branch a year before it produces fruit.
Don't ever cut branches while they are in flower.
Don't let the humidity build up around fruit.
Plants do well if fed heavily in the spring.
Don't heat the greenhouse in winter.

You also need to remember that whatever pruning regime you use, you must have some shoots that will grow leaves but no fruit this year, so that next year they can produce fruit. All pruning takes place at the end of the season when the plant isn't actively growing.

Single cordon vines

Most people grow vines in a greenhouse, so plant your vine outside and train it through the glass to the inside. Allow it to grow unhindered.

The soil should be well dug and mixed with plenty of well-rotted manure and compost. In the summer of the first year allow the plant to grow, and pinch back any lateral shoots to around five leaves.

When the leaves have fallen off in the winter, cut back the main shoot by just a little more than half and cut the laterals to a single bud each.

The following summer, treat the plant as you did the previous summer; tie in the main shoot and build your frame of wires. Take out any flowers that form. The following winter cut the main shoot back to old wood and the laterals to a strong bud each. The buds will then grow out, and the resultant growth is trained along the wires.

In the third summer allow one bunch of grapes per lateral shoot to form, and any sub-laterals that form keep to a single leaf. In the winter, when the grapes are taken and the leaves have fallen, cut the laterals to two buds. It is these buds you will use next year and so on.

> *You have just spent a year preparing your plant ready for producing laterals that you will now tie in the following spring and summer.*

Chemical fertilizers:
There is nothing wrong with using chemical fertilizers to get some old barren soil going, but there comes a time when you need to make sure the soil is in good heart.

This can only happen by the continued application of manure and compost. Over the years you should see the level of your vegetable plot increasing because you put so much muck on it.

The traditional amount is 4 tonnes per acre, which equates to a quarter barrow load for every square yard.

Leave it on the surface in winter and dig what the worms have left in March.

Melons

This is such a wonderful plant to grow, and since supermarkets have been selling them far too cheaply, no one seems to grow them any more.

You need to sow in warm conditions, a heated greenhouse in April is fine. Sow in individual pots, a 3in (8cm) pot is just right. Sow two seeds and later remove the weakest. Sow the seeds on their edge about an inch (2.5cm) deep.

Melons need three important things: excellent nutrition, really good drainage and heat. This way you are guaranteed to get a crop. Keep the temperature at around 20°C. You can sow more seeds every fortnight until June, if you have the room, to get a huge crop from late July to September. I now grow melons much further apart, around 4ft (120cm) to give them plenty of room. When they have their true leaves, it is best to wait for the second sets to appear, then you can pot out into their growing positions in June. You can also grow them in rich compost outside in a warm sunny position. They might need help with pollination, so go round with a soft brush and then give a liquid feed at least fortnightly with the watering (I use tomato feed).

Melon varieties:

Bastion – *a very tasty melon*

Outdoor Wonder – *warm the soil with black plastic*

Sweetheart – *a very early melon that matures sweetly*

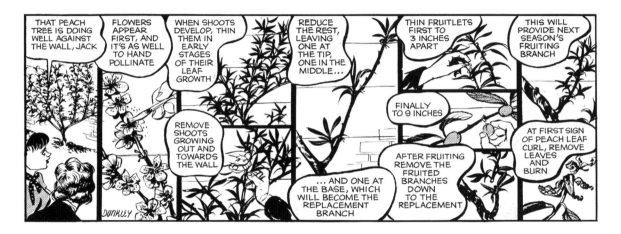

Peaches

A lot of gardeners have started growing peaches because greenhouses and polytunnels have become so much cheaper. The problem was that you really needed a south-facing wall and to be in the south of England. But whichever part of the country you live in, it's best to grow them in a greenhouse, where you are assured a good crop – and the birds are less likely to get to the fruit before you do!

You don't have to plant peach trees in the soil; a large tub is just as good, especially if you are short of room. They need a rich, well-drained soil that can be kept moist but must never stand in water. They like the best of both worlds, moist but well drained. Dig in lots of well-rotted manure and mulch with compost each spring.

Seasonal care

In the winter peaches don't mind the cold at all, but in the spring the temperature builds up quickly in the greenhouse, so open a window for ventilation. Once the greenhouse gets hot, water the floor to increase the humidity a little and when the flowers open give the pollination a hand by brushing with a soft brush. The fruits can rot if not properly ventilated, so remove fruits that are too close together. Feed weekly during the growing season with tomato feed.

Peach varieties:

Bellegarde – *a heavy cropper with extremely large tasty fruit*
Peregrine – *produces medium to large crimson red fruit with juicy white flesh and good flavour*
Amsden June – *a hardy peach*

Free seeds:
A lot of people ask me which is the best magazine to read about gardening. I always answer the same way: the one with most information in it.

Don't be tempted with packets of seeds on the cover, they cost next to nothing for the magazine to stick them on the front. Usually the seeds cost only pennies, even though they advertise them for much more.

Besides, when you buy a magazine with seeds on the cover you are stuck with only that variety and it is much better to go and buy them separately.

The garden can be a dangerous place and there are some pretty obvious things to remember.

Don't leave tools on the floor, you can fall or stab yourself, and even do the old garden rake trick and give yourself a black eye.

Pumpkins - *Great one for the kids*

First of all you need space, at least 6ft (2m) around each plant – more would be better!

Dig as much good compost and well-rotted manure into the soil as you can, as these are hungry plants. Sow 'Giant' seeds in May in pots and keep them warm and moist. (Try the variety 'Volunteer 2004'.)

Pumpkins won't germinate in cool temperatures, so use a propagator and keep them at 25°C.

In June you can plant the seedlings into their growing bed. Place a cloche over them to keep them warm. You can remove this after a week or so. Water at least once a week, with liquid fertilizer.

As they grow, draw soil around the plants to encourage more roots to grow and stop them falling over later when the fruits are large. Sometime in July they will flower and produce fruit. If the stems (also called vines) get tangled or tight, cut some out. Keep on watering and feeding, otherwise the fruit will crack. You can harvest any time after September – the longer you wait the bigger they will get.

RASPBERRIES

I PRUNED MY RASPBERRIES AFTER FRUITING LAST YEAR. WHAT DO I DO NOW?

FOR SUMMER-FRUITING PLANTS

TOP THE NEW CANES SO THAT THEY ARE ALL 5-6 FEET HIGH

AND MAKE CERTAIN THAT SUPPORTING WIRES ARE SECURE

FOR AUTUMN-FRUITING PLANTS

CUT ALL THE NEW CANES NOW TO GROUND LEVEL, TO MAKE PLENTY OF GROWTH DURING THE SUMMER TO BEAR THE LATER FRUIT

AND DON'T FORGET WHEN **PLANTING** NEW CANES TO CUT BACK EACH **JUST ABOVE A LIVE BUD** WITHIN 9-12 INCHES OF THE GROUND

Raspberries

Raspberries prefer to grow in a sunny spot in well-drained, sandy soils packed with plenty of rich, organic matter. Prepare the soil by digging in plenty of organic matter such as garden compost, and removing any perennial weed roots. Most raspberry plants are sold as one-year-old canes. Plant them in the ground and space them 3ft (1m) apart. Cut the canes down to ground level and water well. When they start to show signs of new growth, support them with sturdy posts and tie them in.

Pruning raspberries depends on whether they're autumn or summer fruiting. Summer fruiting raspberries fruit on the previous year's canes. Cut back fruited canes (the woody, brown ones) to ground level after harvesting, to make way for new canes that will fruit the following year. Autumn raspberries fruit on the current season's canes, so they can be cut back completely after harvesting the berries. What's more, regular removal of the fruited canes throughout the season can extend the fruiting period, right into the winter months. They will re-shoot in spring.

Always remember to put a plastic pot or an old tennis ball on stakes and canes and be sure not to tie string where you might trip on it.

Always remember to check the greenhouse glass – I found one of my panes up a tree and it could have fallen with dire consequences.

Raspberry varieties:

There are dozens of raspberry varieties, many of them come from Scotland, where it is more or less the national fruit.

Glencoe – *is a good all rounder*

Glen Moy – *has large tasty fruits*

Joan J – *gives a heavy crop of tasty fruits*

TIP-LAYERING LOGANBERRIES

A CHAP WANTS A BIT OF DAD'S LOGANBERRY, MR D.

YOU COULD TIP-LAYER A BIT FOR HIM

WHEN IT'S FINISHED FRUITING, CUT OUT ALL THE OLD GROWTH

AND TIE IN THE STRONG NEW GROWTH

DON'T CUT ALL THE THIN SURPLUS GROWTH OUT, BUT BURY THE TIPS OF THESE SHOOTS IN THE GROUND OR IN A 7 OR 8 INCH POT BURIED IN THE GROUND, AND PEG 'EM DOWN

ANY GOOD GARDEN SOIL, MODERATELY FIRM, WILL DO FOR THE POT, BUT FIRST FILL IT ¼ FULL WITH CROCKS

ROOTS'LL GROW FROM THE TIP IN A MONTH OR TWO— AND YOU CAN SEVER THE NEW PLANT FROM THE OLD ONE IN THE AUTUMN OR SPRING

CULTIVATED BLACKBERRIES AND OTHERS OF THE SAME KIND CAN BE LAYERED IN THE SAME WAY

Strawberries

I knew a gardener on a rich estate who grew the best strawberries in the world and you could steal the odd one when helping him in the garden, but you'd have to be careful because they were always counted!

There are two possible theories regarding the origin of the name. The older story is that they were called straw-berry because they were grown on straw to keep the fruits being spoiled by the mud. The other idea is that they were once called strewn berries because of the way the fruit seems to be strewn about the plant. Personally I prefer the first – the straw also makes for an excellent deterrent against slugs and snails. Strawberries are grown in many kinds of containers with fruits hanging down, as in hanging baskets, or on pebbles in pots.

Strawberries are very hardy plants. The only time they cause problems is when you have new growth combined with a late frost. Apart from this they are easy growers. They prefer (though it's not essential), a well-drained soil, so put plenty of grit underneath them, and get them into the sunshine, where they can convert sunlight into sweet juice and they're away.

Planting

The traditional time of the year to plant strawberries is in April or May but you can plant them any time except in the frost. If you can, buy from garden centres so you can see what they look like. Too often I have received mangled plants from suppliers by mail order.

Dig the soil well and incorporate some good quality compost and a little grit. Choose a sunny spot and firm them in at intervals of about 1ft (30cm). In May put some straw under their leaves and let them flower away.

Plant the strawberries so the crown in the centre of the plant is at the soil's surface. Too deep and they will be susceptible to rot, too shallow and they will refuse to grow at all. The plants need to be watered every couple of days when first planted, but after a couple of weeks they should be fine. Never water so much as to cause puddles.

Strawberries have a problem with viruses. They get them from greenfly and other insects, though it takes a while for them to succumb. In the first year they are fine, and by the second year they

The thing I worry about the most is the water butt.

I have nightmares of children falling headlong into the water and not being able to get out.

Please make sure you have a secure lid.

are as productive as they will ever be. The third year is a little worse and by the fourth year they are not worth keeping. Fortunately they produce their own replacements.

Runners

The plants quickly push out branches that run along the soil and at intervals, little plants appear. Pop these plants into a pot of compost and place a pebble on the runner to anchor it down. Within a few weeks the new plant is ready to be cut away from the runner. Keep the plant in the pot all winter, preferably indoors, and then plant it out as above the following April.

Varieties include:

Honeoye – *does well in cold and damp*

Pegasus – *fine in wet conditions and stands up to wilts of all kinds really well too*

Cambridge Favourite – *an old variety that is still going strong. It is very sweet and will give you a perfect bed of strawberries*

MILLEPEDES

THESE ANIMALS ONLY EAT ROTTING PLANT DEBRIS MOSTLY...

SO THERE IS NO REASON TO TRY TO KILL THEM. THEY ARE THE GARDENER'S FRIEND REALLY!

Pears

It comes as a complete surprise to people that pears are a fruit made from wood. That slight grittiness you feel when you bite into a pear comes from thousands of little wooded cells called sclerids. They are present in apples too, but are far fewer in number.

The best pears are those which are allowed to grow on the tree until they are fully ripe. They are delicate little fruits which damage easily and for this reason they are grown commercially with tough skins. However, home growers can lavish all sorts of care on their pears and grow softer fruits with little or no damage.

When you buy pears from the nursery or the garden centre, make sure they are certified virus free. There are a number of viral infections from pear blister to a general one called pear

decline, and you could find your stock not doing well at all. There is simply no real way of dealing with these viruses, so the best thing to do is make sure you have certified stock to begin with.

Shape

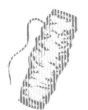

Pears, like apples, are the perfect crop because they can be grown in any number of shapes. A simple standard tree is fine for most people, but you can also think of an espalier – where branches are trained along parallel wires, or a fan, where they are allowed to fan out. This allows you to grow the plant against a wall or a fence taking up little room, but getting the benefit of the shelter and warmth these structures bring.

Pollination follows the same general rules as for apples. The trees flower in early spring and therefore the fruit set might be affected by the wind or frost, or just a shower of rain. You can see why people often prefer to grow them in sheltered positions. You need two pollinators at least, but problems can occur. Triploid pears need diploid varieties to pollinate them, so the best thing to do is to make sure you have at least two varieties available. Another tip is to buy your pears from a dedicated nursery rather than just the garden centre, and then you will get all the advice you need.

If you are used to growing apples then pears will not be difficult, though they are not as quick-growing and they can take a while to respond to pruning.

If you are buying container plants check to see that the roots are not pot bound, and discard them if they are. Bare-rooted trees usually take well. Dig a large hole and give the plant plenty of good compost. Drive your stake in before the pear is planted, as they don't like root damage. A pear tree has a long life, some say up to 200 years, so you only plant pears once and it is worth getting it right. The highest yields come from bush trees, and the best way to grow them is firmly planted in plenty of rich compost.

The further south you are the more readily a bush will grow. In the north an espalier is probably

Companion Planting:
If you want a colourful display in the vegetable garden plant lots of marigolds and nasturtiums.

You might think that plants grow all alone in their bit of soil, but believe me there are lots of roots under the ground and they communicate one plant with another by means of hormones.

Marigolds not only give great colour, but their roots are liked by most crop plants.

You will get a better yield! Also they attract beneficial insects while at the same time act as sacrificial plants for pests like slugs.

At least twice a year you should clean the greenhouse. You need to get rid of all the moss growing between the glass because in the winter it will freeze and crack the panes.

You should disinfect the inside of the glass. If you live near an agricultural suppliers buy some udder wash, because it is the cheapest cleaner / disinfectant you can buy.

While you're at the job, make sure the gutters are free from leaves and that the drainpipe is not cluttered.

Lastly, have a good look around the greenhouse for frogs, especially in October because they like to hibernate there. Give him (or her) a tray of water for the winter — you'll have no insect or snail problems!

best against a wall. Pruning is generally easy. You don't want a crowded bush or tree, so you prune out the various crowding branches. This is normally done in the winter when there are no leaves on the tree. Each spring give the plant a dressing of rich compost and a good handful of organic fertilizer.

Chinese gooseberries -
This has come to be known as the kiwi

Most kiwis come in male and female plants but for some reason the male doesn't do so well here so you are frequently left with huge females with lots of luxuriant growth but no fruit. However, the variety 'Jenny' is perfect because it is self-fertile and produces fruit freely.

Kiwi 'Jenny' is easy to grow. It will grow very large if you let it, so keep on top of her by pruning. Not letting the plant become too large also improves the fruiting. They fruit on one year old canes, and continue to fruit on these canes for about three years. The quantity and quality of the fruit diminishes each year, and you should cut them down to the ground when they are at the end of their third year. The plant should have a mixture of one to three year old canes.

Planting

Plant in a sunny spot in a good rich soil and let the plant grow for a few years unrestricted before you begin to train it. You won't get much in the way of fruit and each spring give it a good feed of well-rotted manure. They don't mind drought conditions and you normally don't need to water until the soil is very dry.

After about six years the plant will be in production and you should be well into a routine of feeding monthly in the summer with liquid feed, pruning at the end of the season and of course, collecting fruit.

Plums and damsons

Plums are simple because once you have got them going they grow all on their own, and for a long time, too.

Plums and damsons flower early in the spring and can succumb to late frosts, so plant them in a sheltered part of the garden, but one where there is good light. You need to protect flowers from driving cold rain, which seems to cause more problems than snow.

The soil should be well draining and before planting dig a big hole, 3ft (1m) across and a couple of feet down, incorporating as much well-rotted manure into the soil as you can, then

Deterring pigeons and mice:
Many of us have tied black cotton from sticks crisscrossed all over the plot to deter pigeons.

They do work but sooner or later the cotton will become a real pest and you are guaranteed to get entangled yourself. This doesn't work for mice, which scurry along the floor and eat what they like.

In my experience most scarecrows don't work that well in gardens and allotments. Perhaps it is because there are a lot of tall objects around so the birds don't think they are human at all.

The very best way in these modern times to deter pests such as pigeons and mice is to cover your young crops with horticultural fleece.

It lets enough light in to allow growth, rain water can get through too but animals have no chance, especially if you bury the edges of the fleece under the soil.

refill. Make sure the trees are planted very firmly and give them a good mulch of rich compost.

Only bury the plant as far as the point at which the rootstock joins the scion, and stake it carefully. Plums are not good with weeds in their early years so once the rain has washed in the compost mulch, give it another layer and even a layer of straw on top of this.

I feed my plums with a good dressing of well-rotted manure all round the tree to a level of 6in (15cm) without touching the tree itself. This keeps it in nutrients and from time to time I give a liquid feed in the summer.

Pruning is simple, you just take out branches that are crossing or rotting and generally open out the tree. If you have bought a plant on a dwarfing or intermediate rootstock, there will not be too many problems.

You harvest when the plums are deep and full. Take one and taste it! You'll soon know if it's ready.

Plum varieties include:

Victoria – *the old favourite, it simply keeps on producing wonderful fruit year after year*
Opal – *a later cropper but it has more disease resistance and it needs a pollinator*
Marjorie's Seedling – *this gives a lot of large fruit, great for cooking*
Czar – *the first truly disease-resistant variety*
Damsons are smaller and more acidic than plums,

making them excellent for jam and cooking and my favourite, a drop o' damson wine.

Damson varieties include:
Merryweather – a good all-rounder
Bradley's King – ripens later into September
Farleigh – a really tasty one, quite sweet

Mr Digwell's Guide to Growing Herbs

Somebody once said that vegetables were more food than flavour and herbs were more flavour than food. I know what he means but it's not right. What is true is that herbs are full of flavour, full of vitamins and frequently they are essential to health.

The important thing about herbs is that they grow easily and more or less anywhere. You can grow them in soil, in compost, in pots on the patio and even on the windowsill. They are not particularly demanding and they don't take up very much room.

It is always useful to have a supply of herbs that you use regularly at the back door and then grow a few others just for the experience of it. I know my patio wouldn't be the same without the sage and lavender growing in tubs. The flowers smell wonderful and the bees just love them. I could sit and watch them for hours!

Buying herbs

There are lots of herb nurseries out there, but you can buy seeds from the garden centre and supermarket. When I started gardening there were no supermarkets and now you can buy little pots of herbs to go with your recipes. Of course they are no use for using straight away, they need planting out in the sunlight and giving a good feed to make them worth eating.

Prepare the ground for herbs

If you are going to make a herb bed you should dedicate around 6ft square (2m²) and plant this up first, making another herb bed later if you wish.

Dig the soil deeply and incorporate at least four or five shovels of well-rotted manure and the same of compost so you have a rich bed. Use the hoe to chop the

soil to a fine tilth. If the soil is not free-draining, add a couple of shovels of grit to every square yard and work in well with the fork.

Which herbs should I try to grow?

Growing herbs is easy, but start with the old favourites which do well anywhere. Lavender, thyme, parsley, lemon balm, sage and chives will all reward the novice grower, and are almost always successful. Try the ones you prefer to use and if all else fails have a go at mint, which you will find impossible to stop growing.

Herbs like rosemary, basil, coriander and marjoram, need more care and better conditions (particularly sunlight).

Starting herbs by seed

In spring sow herb seeds in John Innes soil based compost No 1.
The extra nutrients will see the plants right to their transplanting stage.
Try to sow in modules and plant two seeds to each cell, thinning to one. Cover with a plastic lid and let them grow until they get their second leaves. Keep them warm and well watered, use a fine mist spray rather than a rose.

After germination

The seedlings in the pots are easily transferred to 3in (8cm) pots containing the same type of compost. All you do is fill the pots, firm the compost and then use a dibber to make a planting hole. Push your finger up through the bottom of the module and the plant will come out with a plug of compost. This can then be transferred easily to the pot and firmed in. Water the seedlings and leave them indoors.

Planting on

You will find you have a lot of seedlings, but you can put them all over the garden. Fill in spaces, grow them next to other plants as 'guards' and of course, use them to populate your herb bed. Keep some in reserve in case of mishaps

or disease and then why not put excess plants into hanging baskets or even in larger pots if you wish.

Mint and lemon balm should be planted singly as they take over any other plant that might be growing alongside them. I also find it is important to grow mint in pots even if they are planted in the ground. This stops them from taking over the whole bed; mints are very invasive indeed.

If you are not putting your herbs into brand new pots it is a good idea to give them a wash in garden disinfectant so you do not pass on any diseases and always make sure you add crocks to the bottom of the pot to increase drainage.

Transplanting from pots

When removing the young plant from its pot it is best to do so when the soil is moist. Be very careful not to disturb the roots too much. Make a hole in the final growing position (I use a bulb planter for this) and tap the pot on the bottom with your fingers holding the plant in place. Place the plant in the hole and bring the compost up around the plant, firming in gently. Water well and remember that most herbs grow and spread so make sure they have enough room to do so.

Looking after your herbs

Keep your herbs moist, but protect them from hard driving rain because they don't like to be battered or waterlogged. Feed weekly with an organic liquid fertilizer. If the herbs are takes as leaves, pick little but often, and alternate which plant you harvest. This way you are giving the plants plenty of time to recuperate. There are some herbs, like sage, which prefer to be dry in the summer, but it won't matter that much if you water them.

Pick off any flowers that appear in early summer, as this will make for more vigorous growth, but later keep some to dry, or wait until seeds appear and then store some for the following season.

When the weather starts to get colder, place the pots in a sheltered spot or back in the greenhouse, or bring them into the kitchen so you can easily continue to use them in your cooking.

If your plant is getting too big for its pot, just transplant into a slightly larger pot and top up with some extra fresh compost. This is best done on a bright, sunny day. Again, water well and allow to stand in a sunny spot to recover.

Pests and diseases

Herbs have very strong natural defence from insects, it is all the strong chemicals in the sap that deters them. You do find that snails are partial to sage and I have often wondered if the animal actually knows it is good for them, as though they were treating themselves for a molluscan ailment we know nothing of. Perhaps we'll never know!

Onions, mints and chives get a problem called rust. It looks like rusty marks on the stem and is caused by a fungus. This is common when you grow herbs on soil just rescued from the tyranny of the lawn. All you need to do is cut the rust out and allow the plant to recover.

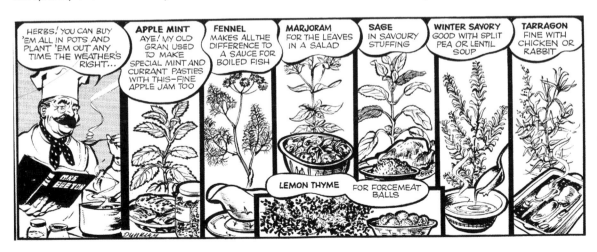

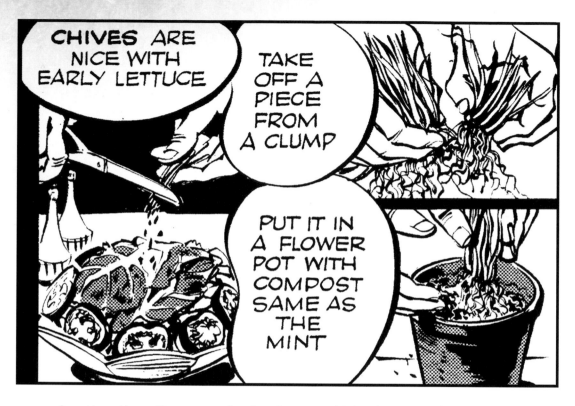

Sometimes they will recover well, other times not; this is why you need plants in reserve.

Don't put chemicals, insecticides and weed killers near herbs. For some reason I feel better if herbs are completely organic.

Chives

These are members of the onion family. They are very smelly and I am putting them around the outside of the planting area for a good reason. Most insects do not like chives and so they make for a great little barrier.

You can eat the whole of the chive, from the roots, which are said to be good for the lungs, to the bulbs which are like mild onions and the leaves which are, well, chive-like.

The flowers are edible too, but also make great garnishes. When the plants flower they look pretty, so they're an ideal addition to the cottage garden.

In the spring and autumn you can just pull the chives up and separate the bulblets that have begun to divide and replant them. This way you get more for your money. The best way of harvesting chives is simply to give them a haircut if you are only looking for some to flavour an omelette or something. Leave the plant in the compost to recover.

Mint

We cannot live without mint in our house. I almost invariably plant mint inside a pot, bury it in the compost and let the roots come through the drain holes. This way you stop the plant from taking over. We have numerous pots of mint about the patio, but this planter is getting some too.

Mint is a very forgiving plant. It needs rich compost and plenty of water but apart from a good sunny position you can forget it. Simply take a few leaves when you need them and leave the plant to recover. It is a good idea to scatter mint in pots all over the patio and make linings for beds in the same way.

Dividing up is easy – simply tap the plant out of the pot and break the roots into two. Then just re-pot and give a good watering. In the winter you can prolong the usefulness of the plant by bringing it into a cool greenhouse.

There are a number of varieties of mint, each of which need pretty much the same care regime:

Applemint – *tastes of apple, and is lovely in tea and sorbets. You can put leaves in ice cubes too*

Spearmint – *the general one for topping ice creams and popping in Pimms*

Peppermint – *the hot one which is used in tea and sweets*

There are also a number of other mints, pineapple and chocolate for example. There are dozens of unusual flavours that you can buy from specialist nurseries.

Parsley

This is a hungry plant needing plenty of well-rotted manure. It has dark green leaves, always a sign of a plant that provides plenty of iron. The thing about parsley is that it makes an excellent insect repellent so it's a good plant for the kitchen door, but also an excellent one for the kitchen too. It's great in soup and fish sauces, quiches, tarts, in fact it is often referred to as a super food (whatever they are!)

There are two varieties of parsley, both of which are treated the same. Curled leaf and loose leaf are both worth growing and they are almost interchangeable in the kitchen.

Parsley takes a while to establish itself: seeds can take three weeks to germinate, and the little pot you can buy from the supermarket takes time to get going. If you do buy in a pot, plant it straight away and don't collect any leaves for a couple of months. The following year

the plant will produce flowers, so you can keep the seeds and sow them on for next year. Give the parsley a good feed once a month with liquid feed and divide it up in autumn.

Coriander

Many people who buy coriander from the shops notice that, on planting them out, they go to seed pretty quickly. This happens because the plant is given freedom at the roots, and this triggers the seeding hormones. This plant is an annual, so you should expect it to seed, but you can still use the leaves. The flowers are brilliant and keep the seed to sow for next year.

Coriander is a member of the carrot family and the seeds sown in the spring produce great plants for most of the summer. It is used for curries, seasoning soups and goes well in salads. The seeds are wonderful for making your own curries, too.

Sow outdoors in May in well-prepared soil and 1in (3cm) drills. The seeds germinate in about a couple of weeks and when they have pushed themselves through the soil you can thin them to 8in (20cm).

Sage

Sage takes a while to establish itself but once it has it will grow year after year without much problem. It is fairly frost-resistant and as long as you feed it in the spring with compost and through the summer with some organic fertilizer, it will provide you with great leaves.

It will grow well in the soil or a container – all it needs is full sun. It doesn't mind dry

soil, in fact it prefers not to be too wet. When you are harvesting sage, pull off a sprig or just a few leaves. Avoid cutting the plant as the sap reacts with iron in the knife.

You can buy small pots of sage from the supermarket. Keep them warm until the last frost has gone and simply dig a hole outside and plant them. By the following winter they will be quite hardy. Sow sage in March indoors and keep the seedlings warm until the frosts have gone in May, then acclimatize them to living outside.

Sage is one of the few herbs that are used to flavour many different foods. Meat – beef, lamb, pork and poultry – are all flavoured with sage. Sausages – Lincoln in particular, but Cumberland and Irish too – are flavoured with it. Various cheeses contain sage too, from simple soft Boursin-type cheeses made with garlic and sage to pressed sage cheddar-types such as Sage Derby.

There are a number of beers made from sage and of course Chinese sage tea is widely used. The Greeks used sage tea to treat tuberculosis.

Thyme

Thyme is one of my favourite herbs. Although wild thyme grows well in Britain, the common thyme we generally use in cooking is a native of Mediterranean countries.

Thyme grows to a height of about a foot (30cm) and has a spread of around a foot too. It is ideal for pot-growing and will remain good to harvest for several years.

Lemon thyme, which as its name suggests has a clean, lemony flavour, can be used and grown in the same way as common thyme, though it goes especially well with strong-flavoured fish like mackerel.

Both species of thyme grow best in a well-drained soil, in a sunny position. A young plant has tender stems and both leaf and stem can be added directly to food, but an older, more established plant has woody stems and it is advisable to remove the leaves from the stem, discarding the latter as it does not break down in cooking. The leaves are easily removed by sliding the finger and thumb along the stem; the leaves should easily come away, and any remaining leaves can be pinched off.

YOU CAN MAKE NEW STOCK BY DIVIDING ALL YOU NEED IS TO TAKE THE CLUMP AND BREAK IT IN TWO HALVES. WORKS ON CHIVES TO 'CHOKES.

Tarragon

This sweetly aromatic herb is most commonly used to flavour fish and chicken, but once again is a versatile herb.

A tarragon plant can grow up to about 3ft and cover a couple of feet in width. It grows best in a sunny spot in well-manured and free-draining soil. Once established the plant needs very little attention except the pinching out of flowering stems as they appear. Keep the plants well watered during dry weather and use regularly to ensure a constant supply.

Tarragon is used to complement seafood cocktails and added to eggs, either scrambled or an omelette.

Lavender

These plants come from southern Europe so they prefer a position that is in full sun and well-drained rich soil. They tolerate drought very well. You buy them as young plants and transfer them to their growing position in autumn or spring. Incorporate plenty of organic material into the soil and simply remove the pot and bury into position. Each spring give it a good mulch of rich compost and during the summer give it some liquid tomato feed.

In the winter give the plant a trim – just to keep it in shape really and stop it from becoming woody and leggy. It will give you many years of happy scented flowers.

Basil

This herb comes from India and has no requirements except for a sunny position. If you can give it a sunny spot it will grow well. Alternatively grow in a greenhouse or in a 12in (30cm) pot so you can bring it indoors.

Simply sow three seeds in a 3in (8cm) pot of moist compost and keep it around 16°C. They will germinate within a week or so and you should prick out the two slowest growing ones. In May you can pot on to the final growing position, which should be warm and sunny, with plenty of organic material dug in for the best flavour. The leaves and stems don't particularly like being wet so always water the soil or from below if you are growing in a pot.

Rosemary

This herb from hot countries in the Middle East prefers a sandy soil. You buy them as small plants and plant them into a sunny freely draining spot. Once in situ rosemary will stay there for a good 20 years or more. Dig a large hole in April, 2ft square (60cm²) and 2ft deep, and fill it with a mixture of 50% soil, 25% compost and 25% sand. Plant your young rosemary in this and give it a little water. From then on only water the plant when the soil is very dry. Between May and September, however, give it a liquid feed, but don't drown it. In October simply trim the plant so it keeps its shape and doesn't become unruly. You can also grow rosemary in a 12in (30cm) pot, where they do reasonably well.

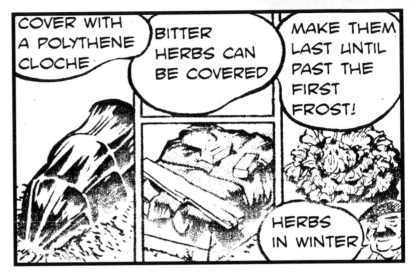

Dill

This is a smashing plant, grown for its leaves and seeds – you couldn't make pickled gherkins without dill seeds!

It is not very hardy, but you can keep a plant going if you bring it indoors in the coldest days of winter. Alternatively, sow by broadcasting seeds on prepared ground in April. The compost needs to be wet and well dug to a depth of two spits (spade depths). If the roots come against anything hard the plant stops growing.

You can cut leaves, which look a little like fern fronds, from June onwards. In July it will start to flower and you can use the whole head in pickles or collect the seeds and keep them dry for later use.

Mr Digwell's Guide to Garden Pests

It's not all-out war

So much has changed about our attitude towards nature in the garden since I started all those years ago. When I was a boy people were at war with anything that ate or spoiled our crops. The idea was to get the most perfect, the very best crops available. Prizes were awarded at gardening shows for perfect produce, with no blemishes or marks and we thought nothing of using every weapon in our armoury to kill or otherwise eradicate any pest that got into the garden.

Consequently, when scientists produced dusts and powders that would kill insects and other pests, we used them, and no messing. But over the years, especially since the 1980s, people have become more concerned with what they are doing to the soil, their food and the environment in general – and rightly so.

So we gardeners are having to use some of the skills of our forefathers when it comes to dealing with pests and diseases because most of what we used to use is either not available, not legal or downright dangerous.

Sometimes we just got it plain wrong. Take millipedes for an example. We

SOIL PESTS

WHEN DIGGING OR TENDING THE LAWN OR BORDERS LOOK OUT FOR THESE

CUTWORMS

DESTROY SEEDLINGS AND INJURE ROOTS

THE BEST THING TO DO IS TO DUST OR SPRAY WITH DDT, BHC OR ALDRIN

LEATHERJACKETS

THE GRUBS OF DADDY-LONGLEGS INFEST LAWNS AND VEGETABLE CROPS

DUST SOIL WITH 5% DDT, BHC DUST OR ALDRIN

MILLEPEDES

FEED ON ALMOST ANYTHING AND DAMAGE ROOTS AND BULBS, AND ARE SOMETIMES FOUND IN LEAFMOULD

N.B. THE FASTER MOVING **CENTIPEDE** IS THE GARDENER'S FRIEND

FORK 5% DDT OR BHC DUST INTO TOP 6 INCHES OF SOIL, OR APPLY POWDERED NAPHTHALENE, 2OZ PER SQ. YARD AND WATER IN WELL

now know they only really eat damaged or otherwise decaying tissue and they hardly ever attack healthy plants. So they are part of the natural decomposing process and we shouldn't be trying to eradicate them.

There are three ways we now deal with pests:

You can pull off the pest with your fingers. This is easily done when you have blackfly on beans for instance, because you can just rub them off. But some people don't like doing this, so you can buy a fast jet spray that knocks them off and kills them at the same time.

Use a biological control method, which is based on the fact that every animal has some other creature that will eat it. So, for example, ladybirds eat aphids. You can get a huge number of biological control solutions to pest problems.

As a last resort, use a chemical. But make sure it is not going to harm the soil or animals you want to encourage. This usually means using organic insecticides and old solutions like sulphur and Bordeaux mixture for fungal infections.

PESTS AND DISEASES

WE'VE LEARNED A LOT ABOUT WORKING WITH NATURE!

Blight

Caused by a fungal infection of potatoes and tomatoes, and is almost impossible to get rid of once it gains control. It will infect a crop with amazing speed, even a day can be too long to leave the plants. It comes in two forms, but invariably is associated with heat and humidity. There is nothing worse than seeing your plants turn black and mushy.

There are two types of blight, early and late. The most destructive is late blight which forms as dark black rings on the leaves. Once you see this, cut off the vines and burn them and then dig up your potatoes, cleaning them in disinfectant, wiping them dry and hoping for the best.

The time to look out is if there have been a number of warm days followed by rain. It might be heavenly for people but it's hell on potatoes. Keep the vines well separated allowing a lot of air to circulate around the plants.

Early blight is not so bad, being caused by a different fungus. You still get black splodges, though not as bad as late blight (which comes from late July onwards). You need to simply spray with a copper-based fungicide, which helps with late blight too, though it is not so certain to clear the crop.

" Don't go into the greenhouse without changing your clothes if you have been dealing with blighty potatoes. Tomatoes get the same problem, only worse, and you will lose your crop. "

There are resistant varieties too, such as Carla, but the best way of protecting plants is to keep the humidity down.

Aphids and ladybirds

Aphids spend their winter as eggs and when the days warm they start to emerge, slowly at first, until millions come along in a rush. The females immediately start to give birth to live females, who in turn give birth to their daughters straight away. The numbers of aphids can explode in just a few hours. They like the tips of plants where they can pierce the sugar filled tubes. Sugar gushes under pressure through the insect and out the other side, making the plant sticky. This is called honeydew, and is loved by ants. It is also a good food for fungi and the plant will become diseased if not treated.

Spray with an organic insecticide, usually based on oils, or treat with sugar soap in a fine jet of water. You can use ladybirds, ladybird larvae and lacewings which will munch their way through a thousand aphids a piece through a summer.

Of course, one completely organic method of dealing with aphids is to rub them out with the thumb and forefinger. This way you are certain to become 'green fingered'.

Not only do the ladybird adults eat aphids, but the larvae also munch their way through quite a few. Keep a colony in the greenhouse or polytunnel. They lay tiny orange eggs on the leaves of plants and overwinter under leaves on the soil.

There are lots of helpful insects in the garden, not all of which you can buy from specialist suppliers. But you can encourage as many of them in the garden as possible.

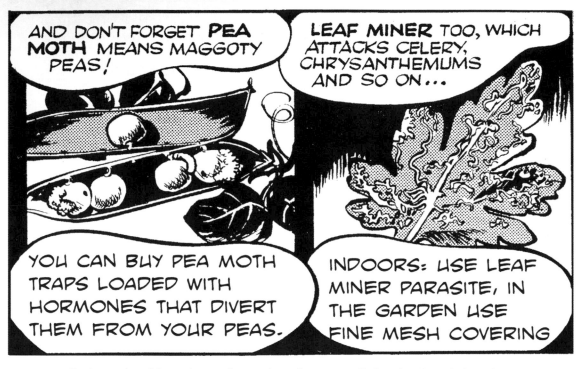

An insect hotel is made up of a number of straws or little tubes in a sheltered position where many insects can spend the winter.

If you can leave a tiny part of the garden a bit less tidy than the rest, and protect it from slugs in the spring, you will find this becomes a reservoir of beneficial insects too. When they wake up in the spring they will become a small army of pest-eating friends.

Traps

Another new way we control pests in the garden is to use an insect's desire to mate against it. At mating time both male and female insects give off aromas that only they can smell and which brings them together. So if you can capture this chemical, you can attract the pest away from your plants and then deal with them without harming the environment in any way.

These are usually called pheromone traps, which you hang on the plants. When the particular insect comes along they are attracted to the trap and get caught in the sticky substance on the card.

Barriers

There are lots of ways of keeping insects off your crops without having to kill them. Enviromesh is a sheet that you simply throw over your growing plants. It allows rain through and enough sunlight to allow the plants to grow normally but insect pests simply cannot get in at all. You don't need to keep the mesh over the plants all the time; mostly during the late spring and early summer. It is very gentle and will not damage your plants if used properly and is an almost 100% effective method.

If you are growing carrots and wish to avoid carrot fly, build a frame around them just 2ft (60cm) high. The carrot fly cannot fly at that altitude and will never get near your carrots. (The same goes for your parsnips.)

One of the oldest and most effective treatments for fungal diseases of trees or any woody

tissue is the product known as lime sulphur (aka sulphur-lime!) It is basically an oily solution of lime, (the same kind you use in the garden) and sulphur. Sulphur, like copper, is an excellent treatment for fungal problems, particularly when it comes to spore-bearing fungi.

You have to be careful not to get this liquid on your skin because it is a severe irritant, and always make sure you dilute it as instructed on the bottle. Otherwise it is difficult to use without problems. Always wear glasses and gloves, and some old clothing.

Similarly, never spray it directly onto foliage because it will kill anything green or delicate.

Actually it is a very safe preparation to use in environmental terms – it kills the spores of fungi and that's that!

Clubroot, as I have mentioned elsewhere in this book, is possibly one of the biggest problems in the gardening world and is in danger of ruining most of our brassica crops if we're not careful. Use much more lime than I said way back. Grow your plants in fresh compost in pots way past their planting-out

Golden rule of pruning:
Pruning is easy, despite what all the books say. You are really only doing one of two things in most cases. You are taking out old wood that has fruited, or you are opening the plant so that the breeze can blow the humid air away.

In both cases you need to remember one thing; when you cut, do it just above a bud and make your cut so the rain, when it falls, will not run onto the bud itself.

If the bud gets too much water it will rot and infect the rest of the plant.

SLUGS

THE BEST PROTECTION AGAINST SLUGS IS **PREVENTION!**

SO KEEP THE GARDEN TIDY AND REMOVE ALL RUBBISH—ESPECIALLY ROTTING GREENSTUFF, OLD BITS OF WOOD, BRICKS AND SO ON

COVER SLUG BAIT WITH A FLAT STONE OR SLATE. RAIN WILL WEAKEN IT

OR BETTER—USE LIQUID SLUG KILLER BY WATERING IT ON THE PLANTS

IF SEED BEDS ARE WATERED THIS WAY JUST BEFORE GERMINATION IS EXPECTED, YOU'LL PROTECT THE SEEDLINGS ALL RIGHT

BUT FOR INDIVIDUAL PLANTS LIKE DELPHINIUMS OR CLEMATIS A RING OF **WEATHERED** SHARP ASHES ROUND THE BASE WILL HELP

AND FOR A SPECIAL PLANT USE A COLLAR OF PERFORATED ZINC PRESSED WELL INTO THE GROUND

date. Then transplant them into new enriched soil with a very good dressing of lime down each hole as I have already described. More than anything else, STOP WALKING ON YOUR SOIL! Your boots will transfer spores all over the garden.

Slugs and snails have always been a major headache. There are so many treatments for them today it is sometimes difficult to know what is best. The use of pellets is frowned on by many, and if you do use them, cover them with a slate. Beer traps work to a degree, but seem like a waste of good beer!

There are a number of preparations made from nematode worms that kill the slugs while they're in the soil. They work as long as the soil is warm, which means mostly using them in the summertime. They do cut down the numbers of slugs and snails a lot, if not completely.

There are a number of barriers for individual plants – copper ones have worked very well, and you can protect a number of pots and containers with little wires on tape powered by a battery.

One of the most devastating sights to a new gardener is a plot full of weeds. Well you can't blame the plants – they're only doing what they do! But there is a lot we can learn from them! For a start, weeds don't waste soil. If it's there they grow in it, no matter how small the patch. Remember this when you plan out your garden. If you grow crops there is always space to put some more in, even if it's only cress.

" But beware: slugs and snails will climb onto plants by doing acrobatics and falling off overhanging plants to get to the food they really want. "

GARDEN WEEDS

YOU WANT TO KEEP THE WEEDS DOWN, BEFORE THEY GET *YOU* DOWN

DON'T I KNOW IT!

ANNUALS
(Hoe these in)

SHEPHERD'S PURSE   CHARLOCK   SPEEDWELL   CHICKWEED   GROUNDSEL

DON'T LET 'EM SEED — HOE OFF WHEN YOUNG OR HAND PULL IF OLDER. DIG IN WHEN GROUND'S TURNED OVER

PERENNIALS
(Dig these out)

DOCK   BINDWEED   MARE'S TAIL   TWITCH OR COUCH GRASS   GROUND ELDER

DEEP DIGGING'S THE ONLY CURE, AND **BURN** EVERY SCRAP OF ROOT YOU CAN FIND — *NEVER* DIG INTO THE GROUND

❝Burning plants instead of composting them isn't wasteful. The ashes are always full of nutrients and you can enrich your compost heap with them.❞

There are lots of ways of dealing with weeds and you can take a choice from using a modern herbicide to more organic ways of removing them. Remember, if you do use a modern herbicide, to wait for the appropriate time before you plant anything in the soil. I would suggest that you learn more about your soil if you dig the weeds out. It doesn't have to be too time consuming or demanding if you work in segments. The problem comes when you have a garden that is a mixture of annual and perennial weeds, so you're probably best simply digging out the lot and burning them.

One easy way of ridding yourself of weeds is to make raised beds. The soil inside the bed area can be removed and piled upside down in an area laid aside for the purpose. For each layer of plant-ridden soil, add a thick layer of fresh manure, then another layer of weed-loaded soil, and more fresh manure and so on. Then cover the lot with a tarpaulin or thick plastic sheet and leave it for a year. You will get fantastically rich soil, and you can fill your beds with compost next year.

Dig out the roots of perennial weeds. They will only grow again and are usually packed with starch so even a small piece has enough stored energy to grow into a new plant and pop up. The tool of choice is a garden fork so you don't continually slice the roots when you dig into the soil.

Garden with nature not against it

In all my years of gardening I have learned only one major lesson, but it's a big one. Gardening with nature is more productive and better for the environment than trying to grow crops against it. All plants want to grow and that goes for out crop plants too! So get them in the soil, even if they're a bit late – they will still grow! If we treat our gardens as something we need to dominate, continually spraying them with chemicals to keep them sterile and pristine all the time, we will be disappointed. There will be less crops, fewer frogs and toads and the birds will pass the garden by as an uninteresting, even dangerous place.

But if we garden with nature, encourage insects (both beneficial and otherwise) and provide a pond for frogs and newts and encourage pollinating insects not only will we understand our gardens better, we will enjoy them more too. And of course our crops will be better for it.

Mr Digwell's Gardening Techniques

Compost

Composting is an important way of putting minerals and structure back into the soil. But you must remember that you cannot simply continue to take from the soil year in and year out without putting something back – and the amount you put back is important, too. Let me explain: if you grow a cabbage in a pot and compost the roots but eat the leaves then the minerals in the leaves will have been lost. You need to compost more plant material than you grow if the soil is to maintain its fertility.

The more you can get into your compost heap the better. Sweep up leaves, add any vegetables you leave in the kitchen that you bought from the supermarket, compost grass, newspaper, cardboard – anything with plant material in it, but not meat, fish or gravy. There are many different ways of making compost and indeed composting has become big business over the last few years as many people have tried to green up their gardens. Some composting systems involve the use of worms, constant aeration, special chemicals or a combination of these to speed up the composting process, but the old method relies on getting the material hot.

Compost should be hot, though there are plenty of composting methods that do not use heat. If the compost is cool then bacteria and other micro

organisms can grow to high levels, and if you happen to be growing something nasty in there it won't be killed without heat. Only a temperature over 70°C will kill these bugs, and hot composting attains these temperatures within a few weeks. A hot heap also kills weed seeds, invasive perennial plants put into the heap and many other things, so try to get your compost hot!

I remember having a compost heap at college that was 6ft high and steamed winter and summer. We used to keep our drinks on it to keep them warm – we could keep a cup of tea warm all morning if necessary.

The basics

A heap is a living thing, and there is a lot going on inside it. Like all living things it needs water, air and oxygen to remain healthy. And as I have said, it needs to be hot – in the centre, not at the outside.

You should water once a month in the summer: just collect a bucket of water and keep it in the greenhouse to warm it. Sufficient air is important, too, and you get this into the heap by turning it over. Initially this will cool it down but gradually the heap will get hotter still. A heap should be turned over every three months.

Two identical bins with a removable centre division between them will allow you to easily turn the compost over by forking it from one side to the other.

The heap needs to be insulated to keep the heat in. Most modern bins do not allow for this, so cover it with old carpets and bubble wrap – anything to keep the heat in. You can make a heap from old wooden pallets which have air spaces, and you should wrap something around these to get the heap hot.

Starting off

It takes a while for the heap to get hot. A good few buckets of plant material is needed to get it going and perhaps some compost starter. You can buy these from garden centres, or you can inoculate the heap by adding compost or a little soil. My personal favourite is a fist full of already rotted compost from another heap and a pint of urine. Some recipes call for stale beer, but for some reason we never seem to have any of that!

Adding material

When you add new material to the heap, do not keep on taking the lid off just to add a little: save up until you have a bucket full, then add that in one go.

What to add

A hot heap will kill anything, but perennial weeds can be added once they have been killed. I put them on a fire for a few minutes first. The powerhouse at the centre quickly becomes fairly sterile as the rotting process radiates out from the centre. This is another reason why it is important to mix your material, to give the outermost material a chance at the heat treatment.

What not to add

I avoid adding any diseased plant material to the heap as an extra precaution because although the heat should kill pathogens, you never can be quite sure. I usually burn these but then add the remaining ash to the heap, or the onion bed.

If you are going to add lawn mowings, add some newspaper, then a layer of grass about 3in (8cm) thick and then more paper and so on.

The nose test

Compost should be sweet smelling, and if you have material uniformly crumbly with a good aroma, you have finished. If it begins to smell bad, then give it a stir, add some paper and green stuff and maybe a pint or two of water and cover it up.

John Innes compost

This is a series of traditional compost recipes, named after a London merchant who gave land solely for research into horticulture. The centre that was built on his land worked on how to grow plants and came up with a recipe for the best compost for plant's growth.

There are basically four recipes: as easy as 1, 2, 3!

J.I. No. 1 for large seeds and any plants you will prick out.
J.I. No. 2 for putting young plants into.
J.I. No. 3 for mature plants.

It was designed so that you start with J.I. 1 and then go on in stages.

To make your own John Innes composts first of all mix seven parts of loam (good quality soil), three of peat substitute and then two of sand.

J.I. Compost No. 1 Fertilizer to add per 1 cubic metre of mix.
1lb (0.5 kg) ground limestone,
2 lbs (1 kg) hoof and horn,
2lbs (1 kg) superphosphate,
1lb (0.5 kg) potassium sulphate.

J.I. No. 2 has twice the amount of ingredients, except ground limestone, and similarly J.I. No. 3 has three times. You will notice these recipes are not organic, but they have been in constant use for nearly 100 years.

The John Innes composts nos 1 to 3 are basically recipes that are guaranteed to give good results. Many people think these are brands of compost, which is not the case.

Making leaf mould

Take advantage of all the leaves falling from the trees and sweep them up each autumn. You can just add these to the heap if you like, but leaf mould is a very fine compost in its own right. You need to pile them into a wire mesh cage and leave them for a year to rot down.

Controlling humidity

There was a school of thought that said splash water around the greenhouse to help with pollination and growth. I have never understood this because the greater the humidity the more chance you have of your plants being eaten by fungi. Most botrytis and mould grow in hot, humid conditions.

To cut down the humidity ensure good ventilation and place a pot in the soil near the plant so you can water without having to splash everything – especially the leaves!

Dividing

Plants in pots soon take up all the room and something needs to be done for them. You can pot them on, but often you can divide them. Simply remove the plant from the pot and using two hand forks as a lever, break the mass of roots into two equal halves. You can do the same with plants in the garden too; just use two garden forks to do the same job.

Remember to give the plant a good watering in new rich soil.

Forcing

You can bring on a plant by keeping it in the dark. The lack of light makes the plant react as though it was at the bottom of a pile of competing foliage, making it grow

quickly and become large. But be careful: the plant needs sunlight at some
time to survive.

The same technique is used on rhubarb to get some long stems in the early spring and
also to make plants like endive rid their leaves of bitter flavours. So long as you don't overdo
it you can't go wrong.

Mulching

The best kind of mulching adds nutrients to the soil as well as covering the land to slow
down the evaporation or loss of water. When it rains some of the nutrients are washed out
of the mulch and into the soil. There are lots of suitable materials – perhaps the strongest is
well-rotted manure. Just don't let it touch the plants. Good quality compost works as well.

Mulching with compost and manure does not suppress weeds, which grow through the
material, but you could put a circle of garden membrane down and lay your mulch on top
of this. The membrane allows water, and therefore nutrients, through, and will be invisible
under your mulch.

Whichever way you mulch, top it up from time to time as the season progresses to be
sure it is perfect.

Using growbags

These bags are perfect for growing tomatoes – which is what people mostly use them for. Don't buy the cheapest ones, which are filled with the poorest compost. What you have to remember is that they need good drainage holes in the bottom otherwise your plants will become waterlogged.

Who says you have to put them in the greenhouse? If you have no other room to plant anything why not place them at the edge of your path? You can put them at the bottom of your wall, too.

Then, who says you have to use them flat? You could stand them on their small edge and slice the top edge. The bag is now perfect for growing carrots. This way you can grow parsnips too – but you'd have to make sure it is well insulated in the winter – bags get a lot colder than soil and you could kill your plants in a heavy frost.

Sowing seeds

There has been a huge change over the years in sowing seeds. Way back we used to use little wooden boxes the same size as a sheet of paper into which we would sow our early seeds and keep them in the greenhouse or a warm potting shed. But now there are all sorts of tailor-made systems for starting seeds.

Propagators come in various shapes and sizes. The simplest is just a plastic box with a clear plastic sheet lid. The lid creates a micro greenhouse in which the seedlings will not be bothered by changes in temperature, cooling draughts and inquisitive fingers. The lid also keeps the compost from losing moisture, cutting down the number of times you have to water them.

Module propagators have the lower tray divided into single compartments, usually 36, which you fill with seed compost and sow one or two seeds in each. You then thin these to one seed per compartment, otherwise known as a module.

When it comes time to transplant the seedlings, you simply push your finger into the bottom of the module and out pops the plant, compost and all! This is frequently referred to as a plug, and the modules are often called plugs too. You normally buy plugs as a special way of sending young plants through the post, usually in a modified kind of module.

WHEN THE FLOWERS APPEAR, ENSURE GOOD RESULTS BY POLLINATING THE FEMALE BLOOM [THE ONE WITH THE TINY MARROW ATTACHED]...

... BY PRESSING THE PICKED, HALF-DAY OLD, MALE BLOOM INTO IT, GIVING IT A LITTLE TWIST TO DISLODGE THE POLLEN

Pollinating

Plants like melons and squashes and courgettes often need help in pollinating. This also applies in the greenhouse, especially in winter, when there aren't so many insects around. There are a number of ways of improving your chances of a good crop.

For things like tomato, just tapping the vine does the job, but you can use a brush. Where you have male and female flowers you can simply pull off the male and use it to pollinate the female.

SOWING THE SEED (3)

OHO! GETTIN' BUSY ON A SEED BED, EH, MR NEWCOME?

YES, THE WIFE WANTS HER OWN VEG, MR D.

WELL, YOU'RE OFF TO A GOOD START—THAT GROUND'S FORKED OVER JUST RIGHT...LIGHTLY, 2-3 INCHES DEEP

THE SOIL NICE 'N' CRUMBLY TOO—BUT GET RID O' THEM ODD CLODS AND STONES

PLAN YOUR ROWS SO THE PREVAILING WIND BLOWS **ALONG** 'EM ...

...THEN THE PLANTS WILL PROTECT EACH OTHER

STRETCH A LINE AND SCRAPE OUT A SHALLOW TRENCH SUITABLE FOR THE SEEDS YOU'RE GOING TO SOW...

...THE DEPTHS **VARY,** SO READ ALL ABOUT IT ON YOUR SEED PACKET

"And remember! A drill isn't a hole, but a row in a straight line. In the army we did 'drill' which was practising how to stand in a straight line!"

Pricking out

As young seedlings grow they need more room and more nutrients. This means they are to be taken from their compost and placed into fresh, sometimes in a pot rather than a tray.

The first thing to do is to make holes with a dibber, ready to receive your seedling.

Holding the leaf only, and taking great care, use the dibber to lever the seedling out of the compost. Using the dibber as a guide, carefully lower the root into the pre-prepared compost.

Carefully firm the new seedling in place with the dibber – gently! Give a water with luke-warm water from a very fine rose.

Pruning

Whatever regime you choose for your pruning activities, always have a golden rule in mind. When you cut, do so just a short distance above a bud. Make it a slanting cut so that if the rain falls it will roll away from the bud.

The seedbed

Getting the right soil for sowing seeds outdoors is an important and sometimes daunting task. You can use a rotavator for speed, but don't overestimate how much hard work using one of these machines can be. Sometimes a good, sharp spade is easier.

Fork in as much compost as you can and remove all the stones you find. Then you can lightly fluff up the soil with your garden fork in tiny whispy movements. You are trying to get air into the top six inches of soil. Then rake up the top couple of inches with a garden rake to make a lovely fine, billiard table surface.

Always plant the seedbed with plenty of space for you to get to the plants to move them on to their final growing positions, and use a garden line to mark out the rows and use a drag hoe to create the drills.

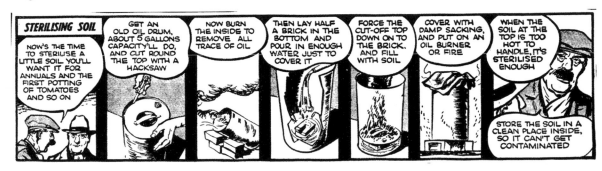

Sterilizing the soil

How easy is it to sterilize soil these days? For a start you will find it almost impossible to get your hands on an oil drum in which to make a steamer! If you have a BBQ, you can simply cook soil on trays on top of it, or as a last resort you can use the oven as long as the missus lets you! Another way to sterilize soil is to have a bonfire on it and then take up the top few inches and pass it through a riddle. Not only will it be sterile but it should also be enriched with phosphates from the fire.

Storing and Preserving What We Grow

The problem with the vegetable plot is that you get too much produce all in one go, and you simply have to do something about it. Mostly vegetables can be preserved by a variety of means, but you often lose the flavour, or significantly change the look of them. But on the other hand you do make some wonderful foods.

There are six basic ways to preserve food: cooking, salting, pickling, freezing, drying and sugaring. There are many variations of these, just as there are a number of pleasant foods we can make that are almost nothing like their original vegetables and fruits. There are even some fruits and vegetables that need no looking after at all, providing you keep them dry and out of the way of vermin.

Ploughman's pickle

This recipe is about taking bits and pieces from the bottom of the vegetable tray and making something of them. There are no real quantities in this recipe except for the vinegar and the sugar. You chop away at the produce to make small pieces, or grate them or you pop them in the food processor. There are some important ingredients; apples, dates, garlic perhaps, maybe some onion or leek. The rest don't matter, you can add anything.

Ingredients can include:

Carrots, peeled chopped into 5mm (¼in) cubes
1 medium swede, peeled and chopped into 5mm (¼in) cubes
4–5 garlic cloves, peeled and finely chopped – or you can grate it
125g (5oz) dates, very finely chopped
2 onions peeled, finely chopped
2 medium apples, chopped into 5mm (¼in) cubes
15 small gherkins, chopped into 5mm (¼in) cubes
Dark brown sugar
1 teaspoon salt
4 tablespoons lemon juice
Malt vinegar
2 teaspoons mustard seeds
2 teaspoons ground allspice (this is what makes it taste like the shop bought stuff).

Chop the vegetables and then add your vinegar, just to the top of the veg. Measure how much vinegar you added and then add half as much by weight of sugar. So if you added 20oz of vinegar, add 10oz of sugar.

Combine all the ingredients in a large pan and bring them to the boil slowly, making sure that everything is completely mixed. When the pickle is boiling, reduce the heat so that it is just simmering and keep this temperature for around two hours, stirring every few minutes or so to make sure the bottom of the pan doesn't catch and the pickle remains well mixed. You can add a little water if the mixture is becoming too stiff.

When the vegetables are just becoming soft you can spoon the pickle into sterile jars. If you leave it for a week or so the flavours will have developed to make the ploughman's flavour.

Pickled beetroot is different from ploughman's pickle because you pour the

pickle mixture over the boiled beetroots, which should be germ free.

Make sure, in all your pickling, that you are completely clean, that all your jars are sterile and that you do not handle the food. Your lids should be self-seal and, if you use Kilner jars, make sure the rubber seals are of good quality. Never use pickle jars for anything other than the particular type of pickle it originally contained because the taint is quite strong.

Pickling onions and shallots

This is easy! It's just that I couldn't stop crying until I discovered that if you prepare the onions under water they don't affect you. Peel your shallots and soak them for 24 hours in a brine solution. The brine is strong enough when an egg floats in the water.

Prepare your vinegar by adding pickling spice, or you can buy it ready-made in large jars. Then dry the shallots and put them in jars covered with the vinegar. They will last until Christmas, when they will disappear quite quickly.

Clamping potatoes and other vegetables

You can store potatoes in a clamp, which is basically a hole in the ground lined with straw. Simply dig a hole big enough to house the potatoes and put a good six inches of straw on the bottom. Make sure the potatoes are dry and in perfect condition. Then you carefully pile the potatoes and cover the lot with at least a foot of straw. Put a piece of plastic over the straw and on the top of this make a mound of soil to seal the potatoes in place.

To retrieve the potatoes you scrape away the soil and take what you need.

Never get them on a rainy day.

Clamping other vegetables can be done using exactly the same process. Carrots do well in a large box of sand. Put a layer of dry sand in the bottom and then alternatively layer carrots and dry sand until the box is full or the carrots used up. A lid keeps the moisture out. Dried, spent compost is another good material for clamping.

Shelving

All vegetables will store for a month on a shelf, some even longer. Apples, for instance, can be wrapped in newspaper and eaten up to three months later. The important thing is that they are kept dry, that they do not touch each other and are free from vermin. Only store perfect examples – use up the rest. The room should be cool and dark.

Salting

This is an ideal method of keeping beans or any other thin vegetable with a high water content. You cannot salt thick vegetables because the salt won't penetrate to the centre. All you have to do is simply to layer salt and the food so that each piece is completely surrounded with salt. Under osmotic pressure the salt draws water from the vegetable and from any living thing in the jar too. You can keep salted products for years, but you have to get the salt out before you can eat it, which means soaking in many changes of water.

"Tala"

KITCHENWARE and ICING EQUIPMENT

- IDEAL FOR THE EXPERT
- A BOON TO THE BEGINNER

42 DIFFERENT TUBES

Saving seeds:
At the end of the season, why not save some of your seeds for next year? I usually keep a few onion seeds back from plants that are two years old. I keep some beans and peas too and have been quite successful I haven't done so well with tomatoes though.

Only keep seeds for a single year and dry them out in paper before bagging them up in envelopes. There was a time when little paper seed envelopes were commonplace.

One more thing: Don't try to save any seeds from F1 hybrids. They are usually sterile or completely different from their parent stock.

Chutneys

This method of preserving is almost like salting but instead of using salt as a preservative you use sugar. In this case the fruit (or vegetable) has to be cooked in sugar and then bottled in sterile conditions. Sugar is not as good a preservative as salt, so you have to ensure that there is enough preserving material in the food, and the jars have to be completely sterile. Once opened the food needs to be consumed fairly quickly.

Drying

Drying is the most basic preservative. Onions, for example are left to cure on a tray. What actually happens is that the outer leaves dry while those inside become waxy. When this has happened they can be layered on shelves or tied together.

All the pulses will dry nicely and can be stored in glass jars. You can leave them on the vine if you like, but I prefer to take them off and dry them on trays in the sunlight of the potting shed window. Don't force them with extra heat; they will manage quite easily. Then just store them in the jars.

Tomatoes dry with a little extra help and the flavours intensify. You can use a solar-powered desiccator, which is really the cold frame with the lid on. Slice them lengthways and leave the sun to do the rest.

Bottling

This method relies on the fact that the fruit has been cooked and hence the germs removed. You boil the food, then put the pieces in sterile bottles and pour boiling water over them, screwing the lid in place while the water is still very hot. The only possible way the food could spoil is if the fruit is improperly cooked. When it comes out ready for use it is best used as pie or cooking material, and is frequently enhanced with the addition of sugar.

The Greenhouse Year

For the serious vegetable grower, the polytunnel, like the greenhouse, is fantastic for growing a lot of produce when the season outside has finished. The two structures have different properties – mostly related to the way the materials respond to their environment. There are things you can do with a greenhouse that you can't easily do in a polytunnel, and the reverse is true also.

One advantage of polytunnels is that they're a lot cheaper than glasshouses. A 20ft greenhouse is at least twice the price of a polytunnel and it would need expertly made foundations as well as careful siting and planning.

Polytunnel and lots of crops

The polytunnel is a cheap way of covering a large area for growing. In effect it takes your plot and moves it 1,000 miles towards the equator, making it possible to grow plants not normally available and, more importantly, gives you plenty of

space to grow large numbers of plants for longer – extending the growing season by several months in the year.

The greenhouse, being more expensive, is more useful for starting plants off ready for transplanting outside when the weather has

warmed, or growing a limited number of plants through the summer
such as tomatoes.

January

Make sure there are no draughts and check your insulation is in place and
hasn't fallen off. I use bubble wrap available from garden centres. Make sure all
the windows are locked up and the seals are secure. The minimum temperature
inside should be 4°C. Make sure you have a good min / max thermometer so
you can judge what is going on inside the greenhouse. I have two, one inside
and one outside.

February

It's time to start sowing in earnest. You can start off tomatoes in propagators,
cucumber, more tomatoes, courgettes, more onions and parsnips in modules so
you can put them into the soil with a head start.

Clean the gutters and check the glass prior to the high winds of March.
Check the automatic window opener, if you have one, and give the seals to the
door and windows a clean.

Put seed potatoes in boxes to start the chitting process.

March

On warm days start to ventilate the greenhouse more because it is surprising
how quickly the temperature rises. Also make a regular check from now on for
pests such as red spider mite and aphids. Start off peppers and tomatoes if you
haven't done so already.

April

Start off sweetcorn in modules or pots. Start a regular watering regime, especially
for plants in pots. Continue with the heater just in case there is a sharp
frost. This applies to temperature-sensitive plants such as celery, courgettes,

cucumbers, dwarf and climbing French beans, marrows, pumpkins, runner beans, squashes and tomatoes.

May

Continue to ventilate the greenhouse and water plants. You might need to water twice a day – be careful not to splash it about. Keep a watering can indoors so it warms up for watering without shocking the plants. Think about shading the greenhouse with whitewash or screens or by growing beans on the outside.

June

Keep on top of the pests and make sure your automatic window openers are working properly if you cannot open the window. The plants need to be watered possibly as much as twice a day. Keep on feeding the tomatoes and other growing crops with half strength fertilizer at least once a week. If you have any growbags, give a little extra compost over the holes.

July

Continue to ventilate and maintain the supports of various plants such as melons, tomatoes and cucumbers. Try to keep water off the leaves and keep the humidity under control. Spray crops with a weak solution of Bordeaux mixture to combat fungal diseases.

August

In the evenings close the windows and look out for cold nights. Bring in pots of plants growing on the patio so that they don't get cold in the evening. Wash off the shading and slow down the watering of tomatoes as the fruits ripen.

September

Continue to reduce watering and once crops are taken clean the compost and area around where they were growing. Close the greenhouse at night and look at the temperature. If you are starting plants for Christmas and later, keep the temperature at 4°C.

October

This is the time for making sure that the greenhouse is completely cleaned. Use a gardening disinfectant and clean everything from the glass to the gutters. Make sure all the staging is cleaned and if you are able, light a sulphur candle to fumigate the greenhouse. Do not enter the greenhouse for a few days following the burning of the candle as it's not good for your lungs. Clean out your heaters and make sure they are working.

November

The insulation can be put back against the windows and make sure the pots and various other tools in the greenhouse are disinfected. You can start off some summer plants, and fill the greenhouse with successive sowings of all kinds of salads.

December

Continue to sow salads in trays for immediate use. Consider digging a hot bed and on Boxing Day, sow some onion seedlings.

Growing Vegetables in Small Spaces

Most people in towns only have small gardens and some do not have a garden at all – but that doesn't mean you cannot grow vegetables. You can find space for growing, even if it is inside on the windowsill, or on a balcony a dozen floors high. If you use your imagination, you should be able to grow something.

All you need is some compost, air, light and water. A planter, large plant pot, plastic shopping basket, dustbin, pile of old tyres, bread bin, almost anything you can get to hold some compost is quite adequate for growing vegetables.

And if you haven't got a garden at all, then why not a hanging basket, a window box, a bag in front of the front door?

Salads

You can grow salads anywhere. Simply scatter the seeds on compost and away they grow. Try a packet of mixed salad leaf seeds, which contain rocket and mizuma as well as curly lettuce and lamb's lettuce. Moreover, these are nice to look at too. They will grow happily in a growbag, which you can place almost anywhere.

Chives, onions and garlic

All the alliums are worth putting into a tiny space because they grow so readily. The odd shallot bulb placed among other plants will reward you with 10 more shallots. And if you place these in many different places in the garden you will get a great little crop that otherwise would have taken up a lot of space. You can do the same for all the onion family – even leeks.

French beans

A small wigwam of climbing beans will provide enough for a small family right up to the first hard frosts. But you don't need to grow them in wigwams, they will just as happily grow up a wall from a large tub, or over a fence. They will crop all the summer through and if you feed them well, you will be amazed at the flavour. Climbing beans also attract pollinating and predatory insects and make a good screen to hide unsightly parts of the garden.

Kale

Sow in February on a windowsill or under glass. Harden off and plant out under cloches in late March. As the plants grow you can pick small amounts and leave the rest to grow. In winter the larger leaves can be used as greens and since it is very hardy you can make kale soup right into the following February.

Pak Choi

Forget your cabbages, these brilliant little plants are so versatile they can be eaten raw, boiled like greens, used in stir-fries, deep fried like spinach to make Chinese fried 'seaweed' and generally used just like their huge cousins. The ribs can be cooked like asparagus or Swiss chard, giving you two different vegetables.

Miniature tomatoes

These you can grow anywhere. Indeed there is a new variety from Holland that is now being sold in supermarkets that is basically like the herbs you can buy in small planters. They are tiny cherry tomatoes designed to be brought home and placed on the windowsill indoors. You can pick toms all the summer through if you feed them, and they don't grow too tall.

Planter pointers

If you only have a patio or a yard it can be difficult to grow vegetables because they are so dark. Yards in terraced houses have walls that are so high, throwing

shadows all over the place. But there is something about it.

Build up your planters so they are at waist height, and even higher if you can manage. This has many benefits. Firstly you can mimic the terracing you find in Chinese mountain fields, increasing the area available for growing. You can also get your plants into the light by lifting them up.

Buy a plastic wall greenhouse, the type that looks like a Wendy house. They need fixing to the wall or else they will blow over, but apart from that they make an excellent warm space for growing seedlings and even whole plants. I have grown peppers in one in the past. They are cheap enough to buy a few and they can line a whole wall, or you can build them half size to fit your available space.

One important benefit of growing in these places is that you can take advantage of the shelter afforded by walls and houses. With work you can make ideal growing conditions.

Save as much bubble-wrap as you can during the year to wrap around your planters to protect them from frost. They might look a bit funny, but soil in the ground is insulated from the cold more efficiently than pots are, so if you wrap up your plants they will do better.

Water pots regularly, even when it rains. The soil shares the water that falls on it evenly, but this doesn't happen with containers. In a downpour you might find that the compost in your pots is completely dry. Pots are easy to irrigate with a system of small plastic tubes from gutters and buckets, and needless to say, you should save as much water as you can.

Slugs and snails will still get to your plants, but you can deal with them quite easily. I have found that you can keep planters slug-free by standing them on copper rings. These haven't worked as well on soil, but have been very successful on concrete.

Mushrooms

However much room you have you must make room for mushrooms. (Forgive the pun!)
They can be fitted into the tiniest spaces, you get a wonderful crop and still have compost for growing other crops. It is this way that the small-space gardener really can see how the growing world can recycle materials. There really isn't much waste in a small garden.
You can buy mushroom kits, which will grow in compost quite happily in a box on a patio or in a yard.

From Plot to Plate with Mr Digwell

We used to boil our vegetables to death when I was younger, but now so much cooking has changed. People stir fry, blanch, roast, toast and make raw salads much more than ever. The key to perfect vegetables is freshness and you simply cannot get fresher than to dig something up one minute and cook it the next.

This is the great joy of growing your own and no matter what anyone says you cannot do better. Imagine produce sitting on the supermarket shelf for hours, if not days and compare it to the perfect specimens you have grown yourself.

Why haven't I won any prizes?

To be honest I could have entered competitions where the rules ask for five perfect onions on a plate, or three cut carrots or whatever. But the truth is that vegetables are not for looking at, they're for eating. So, when they come up with fruit and vegetable competitions where they are looking for the best flavoured specimens, I'll be first in the queue with my entries. And I reckon I'd win first prize every time.

My philosophy over all these years is a simple one. Give the plant plenty of food, sunlight and water and it will reward you with great tasting crops.

The other thing is that if you grow your own vegetables you are much more likely to try something new than if you simply buy the same old stuff from the shops. I remember growing okra or ladies fingers. I'm sure that I wouldn't have bought it, but I wanted to see if I could actually grow it, and then of course, I had to cook it to see what all the fuss was about.

When I was young we never worried about food miles and all that, but these days it is important that we all do our bit. What better way of 'being green', as my grandchildren put it, than to get out there and grow some of your own food?

One last point about plot to plate; you can leave vegetables in the ground for longer. It doesn't matter if you take only one potato haulm, or one handful of courgettes, or a couple of tomatoes. You can leave the rest to remain alive and fresh exactly where they are growing. I can't think of a better storage system!

Mr Digwell Today

There is a huge interest in "growing your own" and "living the good life" these days, perhaps because so many people are looking for a more rewarding way of living their lives. Maybe some have found it important to grow fruit and vegetables for financial reasons, others for health and culinary purposes.

Whatever the reason for embarking into a life close to the soil, one thing is certain: what was true when Mr Digwell started all those years ago still holds true today. The various changes Mr Digwell has seen in three generations, all those fads and new techniques that have come and gone over the years, come down to one simple thing – you put a seed into the earth and it grows.

Perhaps the old parable – a seed bearing fruit a hundred-fold – should be a lesson to all of us. There is nothing else in nature that makes mankind such a profit.

The return of Mr Digwell is,

in no small part,

thanks to Mel Knight.